DI

Employment Discrimination

Employment Discrimination

A Claims Manual for Employees and Managers

by
Andrew J. Maikovich
and
Michele D. Brown

with a foreword by
WILLIAM H. BROWN III

McFarland & Company, Inc., Publishers
Jefferson, North Carolina, and London

British Library Cataloguing-in-Publication data available

Library of Congress Cataloguing-in-Publication Data

Maikovich, Andrew J.
  *Employment discrimination : a claims manual for employees and
managers* / by Andrew J. Maikovich and Michele D. Brown.
      p.   cm.
  Includes indexes.
  ISBN 0-89950-436-1 (lib. bdg. : 50# alk. paper) ∞
    1. Discrimination in employment—Law and legislation—United
States.   2. Age discrimination in employment—Law and legislation—
United States.   3. Pay equity—Law and legislation—United States.
4. United States. Equal Employment Opportunity Commission.
I. Brown, Michele D., 1955– . II. Title.
KF3464.M3   1989
344.73′01133—dc20
[347.3041133]   89-42733
                                                                                          CIP

Manufactured in the United States of America

McFarland & Company, Inc., Publishers
  Box 611, Jefferson, North Carolina 28640

To Tom and Shirley Evans
for all the beers,
Broncos and friendship we've shared
AJM

To William H. Brown III
A credit to the legal profession
and his daughter
MDB

Table of Contents

Foreword   xi

Introduction   1

  I.   The Three Acts   5
    Title VII   5
    The Age Discrimination in Employment Act   6
    The Equal Pay Act   9

  II.   Who Is Covered   11
    Employees   11
      ADEA Limitations   13
    Employers   13
    Exceptions from Coverage   14
      Title VII   14
        Religious Institutions and Organizations   14
        Private Membership Clubs   15
        Membership in the Communist Party   16
        Employment On or Near an Indian Reservation   16
        Veterans Preference   17
        National Security   17
        EEOC Interpretations or Opinions   17
      ADEA   18
        Executive and High Policymaking Employees   18
        Apprenticeships   20
        Tenured Faculty Members   20
      Bona Fide Occupational Qualifications   20

Title VII   20
  (1) Sex   21
  (2) National Origin   24
  (3) Religion   24
ADEA   24
Seniority Systems and Benefit Plans   26
  Bona Fide Seniority Systems   26
    (1) Title VII   26
    (2) ADEA   29
  Bona Fide Employee Benefit Plans   30
    (1) Life Insurance   31
    (2) Medical Insurance   31
    (3) Long-Term Disability Plans   31
    (4) Involuntary Retirement   32

III. **Theories of Discrimination**   33
Disparate Treatment   33
  Title VII   33
    Prima Facie Case   35
    Employer's Response   36
    Pretext   38
  ADEA   41
  Evidence of Disparate Treatment   43
    Evaluations   43
    Prior Discriminatory Acts   45
    Timing of Disciplinary Actions   46
    Position Titles   47
    Warnings   47
    Disparaging Statements   48
    Knowledge of an Employee's Age   50
Disparate Impact   51
  Title VII   51
    Adverse Impact   52
    Business Necessity   56
    Alternative Tests   58
  ADEA   59
  Pattern and Practice   61

IV. **Current Issues in Employment Law**   63
Race Discrimination   63

Racial Harassment   63
42 U.S.C. Sections 1981 and 1983   65
National Origin   67
Age Discrimination   71
   Reduction-in-Force   71
   Use of Salary Information   73
Sexual Harassment   74
Pregnancy   77
Religious Accommodation   79
Affirmative Action   83
Height and Weight Requirements   86
Grooming and Appearance   88
   Hair   88
   Facial Hair   89
   Dress Codes   90
Equal Pay Act   92
   Equal Skill, Effort and Responsibility   93
   Same Establishment   95
Retaliation   95

V. **Statute of Limitations**   99
Title VII   101
ADEA   102
   Willful Violations   103
   Age Discrimination Claims Assistance Act of 1988   103
EPA   104
Extending the Statute of Limitations   105
   Continuing Violations   105
   Poster Requirement   106

VI. **Damages**   109
Title VII and ADEA   109
   Willful Violations   111
EPA   112

VII. **EEOC Administrative Process**   115

VIII. **Procedures for Federal Employees**   119
Age Discrimination   121
Equal Pay Discrimination   121
Filing a Lawsuit   121

IX.   Preventing Charges of Discrimination   123
Applications   124
Interviews   124
Evaluations   126
Early Retirement Plans and Waiver/Releases   127
Sexual Harassment Policies   128

Appendix A
Title VII of the Civil Rights Act of 1964, as Amended   133

Appendix B
The Age Discrimination in Employment Act of 1967,
as Amended   157

Appendix C
The Equal Pay Act of 1963, The Fair Labor Standards Act
of 1938, as Amended   173

Appendix D
Comparison Between Title VII, Equal Pay Act and Age Discrimination in Employment Act   187

Appendix E
Charge Forms   191

Appendix F
EEOC Field Offices   195

Case Index   201

Index   203

Foreword

Borne out of the climate created by the march on Washington in 1963, the Equal Employment Opportunity Commission (EEOC) was established within Title VII of the Civil Rights Act of 1964. The agency, however, was only regulatory in nature. Enforcement powers were limited to the Department of Justice and individuals who filed charges under the Act.

This lack of enforcement powers dogged the EEOC from its inception until 1972. As chairman of the EEOC, I testified before subcommittees of both the House of Representatives and the Senate seeking enforcement powers for the Commission. Without this power, I was convinced the EEOC could never take the forefront in the fight against employment discrimination. Fortunately, the court enforcement version prevailed and was signed into law in the spring of 1972.

After the 1972 Amendment, the general counsel staff increased from approximately 50 to 460 employees, half of whom were attorneys. During my tenure as chairman from April 1969 through December 1973, the total number of employees grew from 389 to 2300. The number of Commission offices expanded from 13 in 1968 to 32 district offices, seven regional offices and five regional litigating offices.

As the EEOC grew, so did its influence. Our first major undertaking during my tenure as chairman was challenging American Telephone and Telegraph (AT&T) beginning in 1970. Because we had yet to be granted enforcement authority, we went before the FCC to oppose AT&T's request for a rate increase. We argued that AT&T's failure to live up to its nondiscriminatory requirement under FCC regulations increased the cost of telephone service.

Through a committee consisting of about six or seven lawyers (only one or two of whom had any litigation experience at all), we reviewed probably 100,000 documents supplied as a result of our discovery demands and proceeded to a hearing in which we put on our case. We completed our phase of the case before a hearing examiner.

A second committee was established to attempt to negotiate a settlement of the charges against AT&T. From time to time the committees established by the Commission and AT&T would bog down. I would meet with Bob Lilly, then president of AT&T, and the two of us would gently nudge our committees along. The final outcome was a settlement which gave significant opportunities for the first time to minorities and women in addition to a very substantial back pay award. The settlement document was signed and approved in early 1973.

The success of the AT&T task force was used as a model for the establishment of a group of task forces to attack discrimination on a class-wide basis. Using our increased research resources, we looked at major industries on a national as well as regional basis, and attempted to identify major employers whose affirmative action and equal employment opportunity postures were poor. I signed commissioner's charges against General Electric, General Motors, Ford Motor Company, Sears, and the International Brotherhood of Electrical Workers (IBEW). The thought was to attack these major corporations as we had AT&T on a broad nationwide basis while at the same time identifying employers in the various regions who were significant in terms of their size, number of persons employed and number of charges.

I believe that during this time, major corporations began to develop a respect for the work of the Commission and the ability of the EEOC to handle charges against some of the giants in various industries.

Employment opportunities also had to be increased at the Commission, however. A training program was developed to allow our secretaries, who were in fairly dead-end clerical positions, to transfer over to the professional side. The program encouraged clerical people to be trained as investigators and then progress up through the ranks of investigators to employment levels previously unattainable by secretaries.

Since my tenure, there have been many changes in the operation of the EEOC. The signals coming out of the Washington headquarters in the late 1980's are mixed. There does not appear to be the same total commitment to the rigorous enforcement of Title VII as there has been previously. The areas with the most activity now seem to be age discrimination cases, primarily those brought by white male executives or supervisors, and sexual harassment cases. The number of race and more traditional sex discrimination cases, however, continues to run at a high level.

As chairman of the EEOC, and also as a private practitioner, my experience was that the most common complaint from employers and employees alike has been that the law is confusing. What they really desire is for someone to tell them in plain, everyday English, without all the legal mumbo-jumbo, what they need to know about discrimination. How do we identify it? How do we defend against charges of discrimination?

Employment Discrimination is a practical guide to analyzing and processing discrimination complaints. The book will help both employers and employees to objectively evaluate the merits of discrimination claims in a way which will allow them to reach an early and fair result. This would seem to be a worthy objective for a society that is inclined to believe everything can be settled in the court room.

Title VII, the Age Discrimination in Employment Act, and the Equal Pay Act are discussed in a very down-to-earth, easy to understand manner. The readers of this book will feel they are part of the discussion, rather than the subject of it.

Massive amounts of time and money have been spent litigating and defending claims of discrimination.

The authors obviously believe that while good lawyers get their clients out of trouble, it is the great lawyers that **keep** their clients out of trouble. In the words of the authors, one purpose of the book "is not to prevent all discrimination complaints, but to create a personnel system in which problems can be managed as quickly and as inexpensively as possible." This book goes a long way towards achieving that goal.

Nearly 25 years have passed since the Civil Rights Act of 1964 was enacted, yet the EEOC receives tens of thousands of charges of discrimination every year. The number of age cases and sexual harassment suits continues to grow each year. If the flood of new charges of discrimination is ever going to recede, then employer and employee alike must begin to understand what it is like to be on the other side. This book, written without the generally perceived employer or employee bias, does much to lessen the mistrust between owner and worker.

William H. Brown III

Introduction

In this year alone, approximately 60,000 complaints of discrimination will be filed with the Equal Employment Opportunity Commission (EEOC). Some will result in relief provided to the employee. Many more will be investigated and closed because of a lack of evidence of discriminatory conduct.

What often proves more frustrating to an individual than having a complaint denied, however, is a failure to understand why a decision was made. In some instances, the only information an individual will receive after filing a complaint is a form rejection letter. To these employees, who filed their complaints in the honest and good faith belief that they were victims of a discriminatory act, a typical reaction is to blame the system, the investigator, or both. In many cases, this anger could have been avoided had someone sat down with the individual and explained the analysis behind the decision. Unfortunately, many attorneys and investigators do not always have the time, or take the time, to provide this information.

A second group of individuals who become frustrated by the administrative process are employers. Employers often find themselves frustrated by proceedings that can lead to thousands of dollars in legal fees even if they ultimately prevail. Many employers could have prevented a long, drawn-out investigation, however, had they understood the analytical processes and taken the preventive steps required to defend a case prior to the institution of a charge.

1

The purpose of this book is to provide employees and managers with a background in federal employment discrimination law so that they can understand, even if not entirely agree with, decisions made during the different stages of a complaint. This book is not intended as a litigation reference. There are many legal treatises, the best of which is Schlei and Grossman's **Employment Discrimination** (BNA Books), to assist attorneys with their litigation responsibilities. This book, however, is written for the layman, either employer or employee, who desires greater understanding about the analysis and processing used to resolve discrimination complaints. In this regard, citation to cases has been limited primarily to those of historical impact. Greater emphasis has been placed on summaries of holdings and legal trends.

An additional effort has been made to avoid injecting personal opinion into the correctness or social desirability of court decisions. Trends, therefore, are identified on an informational, not promotional, basis. This task was made easier by the fact that one author is an advocate for employees, while the other is an advocate for employers. Andrew Maikovich is a plaintiff's attorney with the EEOC. Michele Brown is an attorney with a law firm that represents corporations defending discrimination actions. Combining the interests of both parties is not as difficult as it may seem, however. No one benefits from unnecessary litigation.

Three acts in particular have been analyzed. Title VII of the Civil Rights Act of 1964 prohibits employment discrimination based on race, color, religion, sex or national origin. The Age Discrimination in Employment Act (ADEA) prohibits discrimination against individuals at least 40 years of age. The Equal Pay Act (EPA) prohibits discrimination based on sex with regard to the payment of wages. While the focus is exclusively on these federal statutes, an individual should be aware that many state laws parallel the protections provided by the acts, and sometimes provide greater protection. Some states have age statutes, for example, which protect individuals of all ages from discrimination and not just those over 40 years of age.

Despite the fact that one of the tenets of the book is the equal treatment of men and women, references are made specifying only one gender. In most instances, "he," as opposed to "he or she," was adopted for the purpose of brevity. Under the EPA, in which 95 percent of the charges are filed by women, the pronoun "she" is typically used although men also may file complaints under the Act. In all of these instances, the singular pronoun is intended to encompass both sexes.

Without question, employment law can be a highly emotional undertaking. By fostering a better understanding of these acts, it is hoped that parties will be able to more fully weigh the strengths of a claim and thereby reach an early and fair result.

We would like to extend a special thanks to Lanier Williams, Esq., whose enthusiasm and understanding of discrimination law were an inspiration throughout the book.

This book was coauthored by Andrew Maikovich in his private capacity. No official support or endorsement by the United States Equal Employment Opportunity Commission or any other agency of the United States government is intended or should be inferred.

I.
The Three Acts

TITLE VII

Title VII of the Civil Rights Act of 1964 is the federal law that protects employees against discrimination based on race, color, religion, sex or national origin. It is the most widely-used employment discrimination statute, generating 40,000 claims per year, primarily because of the scope of the employment classes which are protected.

Although enacted in 1964, it was not until a 1972 amendment that Title VII provided the EEOC with authority to file actions in federal district court against private sector employers on behalf of individuals aggrieved by discriminatory acts. Individuals have always retained a private right of action once a charge is timely filed with the Commission. Even when the EEOC investigates a charge and determines that no violation has occurred, individual complainants may still file a lawsuit and attempt to prove their claims.

The objects of these charges, the employers, include private businesses with 15 or more employees, state and local governments, and educational institutions. Complaints may also be filed against agencies of the United States government, although federal employees have different administrative procedures.

Labor organizations may be charged with a failure to represent members in a nondiscriminatory manner or as an employer for discriminating against individuals it hires as employees. Employment agencies, which

5

do not have the 15 employee requirement, are prohibited from failing or refusing to refer applicants for employment because of their membership in a protected class.

Although Title VII is broad-based and provides an individual with a fair opportunity to prove an allegation, it also contains various pitfalls for unsuspecting grievants. Many claims are lost because a charge is not filed with the EEOC within 300 days of a discriminatory act (which may even be reduced to 180 days in certain locations). Under the ADEA, the EEOC can file a lawsuit on behalf of an individual up to three years following a discriminatory act even without a timely filed charge. Under Title VII, however, both the EEOC and an individual lose the option of litigation when a charge is filed beyond 300 days. The government cannot bail out a tardy employee.

Time creates the opposite problem once a charge is timely filed, however. There is just too much of it. If a charge is contested by an employer, the EEOC investigation will typically take two years or more. Once administratively filed, Title VII charges can be converted into federal district court lawsuits at any time, with no maximum time limit. Because, unlike the ADEA, there is no statute of limitation for filing a Title VII lawsuit, there is no administrative urgency to complete an investigation within two years.

Individuals not content with the delay may file a private lawsuit after receiving a right-to-sue letter, which the EEOC must provide an individual six months after a charge is filed. Many employees do not have the financial wherewithal to litigate their own claims, however. For these individuals, patience is the watchword.

THE AGE DISCRIMINATION IN EMPLOYMENT ACT

The reason the Age Discrimination in Employment Act (ADEA) was passed in 1967 is best described by the law itself. The purpose, as identified in Section 2(b), is to "promote employment of older persons based on their ability rather than age; to prohibit arbitrary age discrimination in the employment; to help employers and workers find ways of meeting problems arising from the impact of age on employment."

Faced with an increasingly aged work force and a society which places a premium on youth, Congress built a protective shield for workers between 40 and 65, just as it had in 1964 for race, national origin and sex under Title VII. Later it would increase the age limitation to 70, and then eliminate the upper limitation altogether. Beginning in 1986, mandatory retirement for most of the nation's private and public sector was effectively eliminated.

As with Title VII, the ADEA prohibits an employer from discriminating against any individual with respect to compensation, terms, conditions, or privileges of employment if that individual is 40 years of age or older. This protection encompasses nearly every type of employment criteria in existence. In addition to the protections provided to Title VII litigants, however, Congress supplied additional ammunition to its aged constituents. First, it provided individuals filing under the Act with the opportunity to secure a jury trial. Second, it allowed not only back wages as part of a damage award, but also the possibility of double damages if the violation is determined to be willful.

The first benefit not allowed Title VII plaintiffs, but provided by the ADEA, is the option for a jury trial. To the experienced employment attorney, a jury can be the difference between accepting or rejecting a case; the difference between winning and losing.

The contrast between a judge versus jury trial is like the contrast between playing a game before the home crowd or at a neutral site. Obviously, it is better to play before fans who want you to win. It is the same during an ADEA trial. Although jurors literally swear they will be fair prior to trial, it is only human nature to root for the underdog. When elderly, hardworking Sam Neighbor is up against multinational corporation Steel & Concrete, Inc., it is likely that the sympathies of the jurors will side with the employee. It is also easier for jurors, possibly older themselves, to relate to the older individual.

A judge, on the other hand, has years of training at being impartial. The real difference is evident when an employee can prove that he was treated unfairly, but cannot prove the treatment was because of age. While a judge will look exclusively at the ultimate issue at hand—did age influence the unfair employment decision—a jury often will find against the employer because it appears to deserve punishment whether age was a factor or not. That is the primary reason an attorney might take a chance on an apparently weak ADEA claim when he would not touch such a case before a Title VII judge.

The second benefit provided ADEA claimants is the possibility of recovering double the amount of damages incurred. While the criteria for receiving damages will be examined in a later section, this threat of increased damages has its greatest impact in cases which never reach a jury. The EEOC presently settles, prior to trial, over 95 percent of the cases it files in federal court. The threat of double damages is a great motivation for the employer to settle claims, especially when a jury is the reward if it balks.

This is not to say that settlements and courtroom victories are paths to great wealth. LA Law or other television portrayals notwithstanding, litigants in most situations can only hope to return to the positions they would have held had the discrimination not occurred.

And just whom are these charges filed against? The primary targets are businesses employing 20 or more employees. Most of the charges allege that an employer deliberately treated a younger co-employee better than his older counterpart. The older employee either misses out on promotion, is the first to be demoted or is terminated. Other claims include the failure to hire or the receipt of lesser benefits, such as insurance or severance pay.

While employers are the primary targets, unions and employment agencies may also be listed as primary defendants or co-respondents. Unions most often are involved as co-respondents, along with the employer, because of perceived discriminatory collective bargaining agreements. Unions may be targeted as primary employers, however, for discriminating against the people they employ.

Employment agencies, on the other hand, are prohibited from failing or refusing to refer applicants for employment because of the applicants' age. Unlike an employer, which requires 20 or more employees for it to be covered by the Act, one person can be considered an employment agency if that person regularly seeks applicants for employers.

The ADEA is clearly superior to Title VII in terms of protecting employees. The process itself, however, is often long and uncomfortable. EEOC processing, barring early settlement, will usually take from one to two years. The judicial process may be even longer. To those who have the patience and stamina, however, the system will provide a fair opportunity of success.

THE EQUAL PAY ACT

The first civil rights employment act to be passed by Congress, the Equal Pay Act of 1963 (EPA), requires that women and men receive equal pay for equal work. In reality, the statute was designed to remedy the problem of women being paid less than men in the workplace. The Act also may be used by men, however, if an employer pays women higher wages for equal work.

The EPA does not receive the publicity of Title VII, a statute passed one year later. The EPA prohibits only sex discrimination, not race, national origin or religious discrimination. Title VII is significantly broader in scope than the EPA, prohibiting any type of sex discrimination in the workplace, including wage discrepancies. Any violation of the EPA, therefore, is also a violation of Title VII. The converse is not true. Title VII emcompasses hirings, firings and the conditions of employment not involving wage disputes.

There are possible advantages to filing an unequal pay complaint exclusively under the EPA or in conjunction with Title VII, however. The EPA provides the possibility of liquidated damages, or double the amount of actual loss, if a willful violation is proven. Other advantages include the possibility of a jury trial and the lack of administrative processing requirements prior to the filing of an EPA action. An employee can proceed directly to court and file a private lawsuit without ever filing a complaint with the EEOC. This is particularly important to an individual who has missed the 300-day filing period under Title VII, but remains within the two- or three-year limitation period under the EPA.

Under most circumstances, it is recommended that an employee with a sex-wage discrimination complaint file under both the EPA and Title VII. While most evidence used to prove a case will overlap, there are slight differences in the statutes which may be crucial. The EPA, for example, does not apply to certain businesses engaged in retail sales, fishing, agriculture and newspaper publishing covered by Title VII. Probably the most significant difference, however, is the minimum number of employees requirement. Under the EPA, only two employees (one male and one female) are required for court jurisdiction. These two employees need not even be employed simultaneously, but may precede or follow one another. Title VII, however, requires the employer to have 15 employees prior to falling within the jurisdiction of the statute.

II.
Who Is Covered

EMPLOYEES

Employment discrimination laws protect individuals, employees, and applicants for employment. Not everyone who works for another, however, is an employee under the Acts. The plumber who cleans the drains and the gardener who mows the lawn are not employees, but independent contractors. Independent contractors are not protected by federal employment laws.

Just who is considered to be an employee? Title VII and the ADEA define an employee as "an individual employed by the employer." Because the circularity of this definition provides little guidance on the issue, courts typically consider a number of factors when determining whether an individual is an employee under the Acts. Most courts have adopted a test that combines the employer's "right to control" a worker with an "economic realities" standard adopted by the Supreme Court.

The "right to control" test focuses on an employer's right to determine the manner in which work is to be completed. If an employer instructs the individual on how the work is to be completed, the time of day it is to be completed, the equipment to be used or even the breaks that an individual may take, the situation will resemble an employment opportunity covered by the Acts. If an individual is merely hired to do a job, however, and is basically allowed to complete the job in whatever way he chooses, the individual will probably be considered an independent contractor.

The "economic realities" test is closely related
to the right of control. It primarily focuses on the
degree of economic dependence maintained by a worker.
The economic realities test and the right to control
test have been combined by many courts to create
a "totality of the circumstances" test consisting of
twelve factors. While no one factor is determinative,
the most important factor is the employer's right to
control the means and manner of a worker's performance. Other factors of significance include: (1) the
type of occupation involved and whether the work
is usually directed by a supervisor or by a specialist
without supervision; (2) the skill which the particular
occupation requires; (3) whether the "employer" or
the individual furnishes the equipment used and the
place of work; (4) the length of time during which
the individual has worked; (5) the method of payment,
that is, by time or by the job; (6) the manner in which
the relationship is ended, that is, by one or both of
the parties, with or without notice or explanation;
(7) whether annual leave is given; (8) whether the work
is an integral part of the "employer's" business; (9)
whether the worker accumulates retirement benefits;
(10) whether the "employer" pays social security taxes;
and (11) the intention of the parties.

The designation or title given a position is not
determinative of whether an employee situation exists.
The fact that an individual is designated a volunteer,
for example, will not necessarily defeat a cause of
action. Any non-paid position which is primarily used
as a step toward full-paid employment will be considered
an employment situation by the EEOC. And as is illus-
trated in **Doe v. St. Joseph's Hospital of Fort Wayne,**
788 F.2d 411 (7th Cir. 1986), the fact that a doctor
admits that she is not an employee of the defendant
did not defeat her cause of action. What is most important is the actual work relationship established between
the individual and the organization.

By comparison, the totality of the circumstances
test defeated a cause of action filed by grocery baggers
at an Army commissary. The court in **Mares v. Marsh,**
777 F.2d 1066 (5th Cir. 1985), reached this conclusion

because no Army personnel had any role in the hiring, firing or supervision of the baggers at the commissary. The Army did not pay the baggers, report their income nor withhold or report withholding or FICA taxes. The baggers did not accumulate annual or medical leave nor receive insurance or retirement benefits. It was the head bagger, not the Army, that had exclusive authority over the baggers' work arrangements and schedule.

Certain workers are specifically excluded from the Acts' definition of the term employee. Whether those employers control the work of the individuals is irrelevant. Those excluded include individuals elected to public office of a state or political subdivision, members of their personal staff, and individuals appointed to policymaking or advisory positions involving the exercise of constitutional or legal powers of the office. Civil service workers, however, are not excluded from the definition of the term employee.

ADEA Limitations

The ADEA protects employees at least 40 years of age. It is perfectly legal to discriminate on the basis of age against employees 39 years of age or younger. Employees who are 39 years of age or younger, however, and believe they have been discriminated against because of age should check for possible state or local laws in this area. Many state statutes prohibit age discrimination with no minimum limit.

EMPLOYERS

For purposes of Title VII, an employer is any person engaged in a business which affects commerce, as long as certain other criteria are met. The business must have at least 15 employees working each day for twenty weeks in the preceding or current year. The employees may be either full- or part-time, and the weeks need not be consecutive. A business with ten full-time employees for a full year and five

part-time employees for 20 weeks would have the
required number of employees. If the part-time employees worked only for ten weeks, the business would
not be an employer.

To be an employer under the ADEA, a business
must have 20 rather than 15 employees for twenty
weeks.

Almost all employers are engaged in an industry
affecting commerce. For example, the purchase or
sale of goods moved from one state to another affects
commerce. This is true even if a business buys supplies
manufactured in another state from a store down the
street.

EXCEPTIONS FROM COVERAGE

Title VII

Religious Institutions and Organizations

Churches, religious institutions and organizations
are allowed to employ individuals that are members
of a particular religion. A religious organization may
only discriminate with respect to positions connected
with the carrying on of religious activities. It is not
allowed to discriminate with respect to positions involving activities outside its religious mission.

The term "religious activity" has been broadly defined
by the courts. Since determining whether an activity
is religious or secular is often a difficult one, courts
have declared that all non-profit activities carried
out by a religious institution are protected by Section
702. A building engineer at a non-profit gymnasium
owned by the Mormon church, for example, was not
protected by Title VII when he was terminated for
failing to be certified as a member of the church.
Although youth basketball leagues do not appear inherently religious, non-profit activities are presumed
to be a part of a religious mission. Profit-making activities will be more closely scrutinized, however.

Religious educational institutions, whether profit

or non-profit, may employ individuals of a particular
religion if the school is substantially owned, supported,
controlled or managed by a particular religion or
religious association, or the curriculum is directed
toward the propagation of the religion.

While religions are allowed to hire members on
the basis of faith, they are not allowed to discriminate
on the basis of race, national origin or sex. Catholic
males, for example, could not be favored over Catholic
females. The only positions in which a religious institution may discriminate on the basis of race, national
origin or sex involve ministerial or other leadership
roles. The relationship between a church and its ministers has been held to be protected by the First Amendment. For positions not involving leadership, however,
religious organizations may not discriminate against
members of the faith because of an additional trait
protected by Title VII.

Private Membership Clubs

Bona fide private membership clubs are exempt
from Title VII's definition of an employer. To qualify
for the 701(b) exemption, a club must be bona fide,
private and exempt from taxation under Section 501(c)
of the Internal Revenue Code of 1954.

To be considered bona fide, a club must be a club
within the ordinary sense of the word. The EEOC adopted
the definition of "club" cited by Webster's Dictionary
and the court in **Quijano v. University Federal Credit
Union**, 617 F.2d 129 (5th Cir. 1980), which defined
it as:

an association of persons for social and recreational
purposes or for the promotion of some common
object (as literature, science, political activity)
usually jointly supported and meeting periodically,
membership in social clubs usually being conferred
by ballot and carrying the privilege of use of the
club property.

In **Quijano,** a credit union was not considered a private

club, despite its Section 501(c) tax exemption, because
the credit union's purpose was to invest the money
of its members and not for social purposes. Likewise,
record clubs, auto clubs and other organizations created
for the purpose of purchasing goods instead of the
commingling of members will not fall within the exception.

A club must limit its membership. An organization
which allows anyone to join upon payment of a fee,
for example, will not be considered private. Other
factors considered by the EEOC which involve the
privacy issue include the extent to which a club limits
its facilities and services to members and the manner
of advertisement used to solicit new members from
the general public. A club that is usually open to the
public and is financially dependent on public revenue
will not fall within this exemption to Title VII coverage.

Membership in the Communist Party

Employers may intentionally discriminate against
members of the Communist Party or any other organization required to register as a Communist-action or
Communist-front organization pursuant to the Subversive
Activities Control Act of 1950. An employer may
not pick and choose the Communists against whom
it will discriminate, however. An employer that discriminates against male Communists, for example, must
also discriminate against female Communists or it
will actually be discriminating on the basis of sex.

Employment On or Near an Indian Reservation

Indian tribes are exempt from Title VII under section
701(b). Private employers may also provide Native
Americans a hiring preference when the business is
located on or near an Indian reservation. To give such
a preference, the employer must publicly announce
that it is providing hiring preferences to Indians. The
distance required for a business to be considered near
a reservation will vary according to location, but will
basically envelop that distance considered to be reason-

able for a person to travel for employment. Distances approximating 50 miles will be considered reasonable in most areas.

Veterans Preference

Title VII does not repeal or modify any federal, state, territorial or local laws which confer special rights or privileges on veterans. Technically, an employer that provides veterans' preferences on its own accord, not required by law, may impact on females or other protected groups. Employers in this situation, however, have strong arguments that service in the United States armed forces provides excellent experience and discipline important to handling a position in question. A violation would probably be found only if veteran's status was an absolute requirement for employment consideration.

National Security

Section 703(g) provides that any employer may refuse to hire an employee who fails to meet the requirements for a position involving national security. The position must be subject to national security requirements as imposed by a statute of the United States or by an executive order of the president. Employers must also describe exactly how an employee failed to fulfill or ceased to fulfill the requirements which denied him access to a position.

EEOC Interpretations or Opinions

An employer that violates Title VII still may be vindicated if it can prove that it relied in good faith on a Commission opinion letter or interpretation. This does not include discussions with Commission employees or legal staff, however. According to Commission Regulation 1601.33, the only documents which may be relied upon for this defense include letters entitled "opinion letter" and signed by the general counsel on behalf of the Commission or matters published and specifically designated EEOC Interpretations or Opinions in the **Federal Register.**

ADEA

Executive and High Policymaking Employees

While employers are not free to discriminate, they must be allowed to set the course of their businesses. Therefore, in an effort to balance the legitimate business interests of an employer against an employee's interest in being free of arbitrary retirement, Congress exempted from the ADEA coverage bona fide executives and high policymaking employees between 65 and 70 years of age.

For an employer to claim this exemption, it must establish that in the two-year period prior to retirement, the employee worked in a bona fide executive or high policymaking position. In addition, the employer must show that the employee is entitled to an immediate, nonforfeitable retirement benefit from a pension, profit-sharing, savings or deferred compensation plan or a combination thereof, aggregating at least $44,000 per year.

The EEOC defines a bona fide executive as an employee whose primary duty is to manage a business, or a division of a business, where he is employed. Typically, the division would at least be a large local or regional operation of a corporation. It would not include the head of a warehouse or retail store. In most situations, the executive would be located in corporate or regional headquarters where decisions are made regarding the course of business conduct.

In managing a company, an executive must have the authority to hire and fire employees, or at least have considerable influence in their hiring, firing and advancement. The executive must not devote more than 20 percent, or 40 percent for retail or service establishments, of his average work week to activities not related to the discretionary running of the business. The only exception to the above criteria is for employees in sole control of an independent establishment, a physically separated branch establishment, or an employee who owns at least 20 percent of a business.

The high policymaking position exception involves top level employees who are not bona fide executives. Individuals who play a significant role in the development of corporate policy and who effectively recommend the implementation of such policy are covered. An example of a high policymaking employee is a chief economist or chief research scientist who evaluates economic or scientific trends, develops and recommends policy to the top executive officers, and who has a significant impact on the ultimate decision of those policies as a result of expertise and access to the decision makers. An expert or professional who merely suggests new strategies is not covered by the exemption. The individual who has a defined role in deciding new strategies is within the exemption.

One court determined that the chief labor counsel for a corporation was not a high policymaking employee because he played a minor role in developing and implementing company policy. Another court found that an employee who tried to downplay his responsibilities as a senior vice-president was a bona fide executive because he was one of four managers and he had authority to approve disbursements of money.

Finally, the employee must be entitled to or have the option of electing an annual retirement benefit totalling $44,000. The benefit must be available to the employee within 60 days of the effective date of retirement. If the benefits are only provided after death, they are not included in the $44,000 total.

Sometimes a company may find itself with an employee who meets the decision making criteria but is not entitled to $44,000 in retirement benefits. The company is allowed to create another pension plan to meet the $44,000 limitation.

It is absolutely required that the benefits be nonforfeitable. Any benefit, for example, which is contingent on an employee not working for a competitor, is forfeitable since the executive could choose such work. Whether the executive so chooses is irrelevant. A forfeitable benefit may not be included in the aggregate.

Apprenticeships

Bona fide apprenticeship programs are not covered by the ADEA. Therefore, apprenticeship programs are allowed to set age limitations for individuals who apply. Although the EEOC views apprenticeship programs as more in the nature of education and less in the nature of employment, it will scrutinize a program to insure that it is bona fide.

According to Commission regulations a program is bona fide if: the apprentice program is in an apprenticeable trade; the apprenticeship program runs for one year or more, with progressively increasing wages averaging 50 percent of the journeyman's rate over the length of the apprenticeship; the program is registered with a recognized apprenticeship agency; the program has adequate facilities for training and supervision; appropriate records are kept to monitor the participants' progress; and there are at least 144 hours of instruction per year. Apprenticeship programs which do not meet each of these standards will not be allowed to limit participation because of age.

Tenured Faculty Members

Tenured faculty members may be forced to retire at age 70 under Section 12(d) until December 31, 1993.

Bona Fide Occupational Qualifications

Title VII

In certain employment situations, only members of a particular sex, religion or national origin can reasonably perform the duties and functions of a job. While not occurring very often, situations which require a specific class of individuals do not violate Title VII. It is the employer's burden, however, to prove that such specificity is a bona fide occupational qualification (BFOQ) for the normal operation of a business or enterprise.

Congress did not provide a BFOQ defense for race

and color in Section 703(e). It appears that there could be narrow exceptions for even those categories, however. The prime example of a BFOQ is positions involving actors or actresses. A heterosexual couple by definition would require a male and a female. If authenticity is desired, the children would have to be of the same race. It is in this type of situation, in which individuals from only one category can perform the duties of a job, that an employer may deliberately discriminate in conjunction with an employment opportunity.

The BFOQ defense has been interpreted by both the EEOC and the courts very narrowly. It is similar to the business necessity defense offered in disparate impact cases. The major difference, however, is that the BFOQ defense allows an employer to deliberately discriminate while the business necessity defense involves unintentional discrimination. The following is a list of the situations in which the defense may be used in various Title VII circumstances.

(1) Sex. The most prevalent use of the BFOQ defense under Title VII involves employment decisions based on sex. As with other protected groups, the defense may be used only in narrow circumstances. It most likely will be accepted in situations involving privacy and safety. The situation in which it has been universally unaccepted involves decisions based upon stereotypes.

It is not a valid defense to claim that customer expectations or preferences determined the sex of an employee. Prior to Title VII, cabin attendant positions for major airlines were exclusively held by females. Today, male attendants are commonplace. The fact that the public initially greeted male attendants with uneasiness was not accepted as a BFOQ defense. As one appellate court stated, Title VII was enacted to overcome such prejudices.

Stereotyped characteristics have been most often used in an attempt to prevent women from entering certain professions. Any position involving strength is typically filled by a male. Under Title VII, a woman has the right to prove or disprove that she can handle the physical requirements of the job. It is not an acceptable BFOQ defense to merely state that most women could not handle the physical requirements of a job. An employer which refuses to consider one sex for employment must show that all or substantially all members of that sex would be unable to perform the functions of the job. For positions involving physical strength, it is impossible to summarily exclude women.

Other positions historically held by males, such as umpires, bartenders, casino pit bosses and coal miners have been opened to females. Even the employer with a good faith concern regarding the safety of its female workforce may not use the BFOQ defense. The fact that an area may be unsafe for women at night is no excuse for denying females the right to work the late shift. Every woman has the right to make this determination for herself. Likewise, an employer may not claim that the language is too harsh or the conditions so unpleasant that a woman would not tolerate them.

Although most have already been invalidated or are no longer being enforced, state laws regulating women in the workforce are not valid defenses. Many states at one time had laws limiting the number of hours a woman could work in certain situations. These state laws, when in conflict with Title VII, are superseded. Likewise, when a state law requires separate restroom facilities for the sexes, it is not a valid BFOQ defense to claim the cost of complying with the state law would be excessive.

By now it should be clear that there are very few positions in which women can be summarily rejected. There are three specific circumstances, however, in which sex may be a valid BFOQ. In the first instance, same sex role models may prove to be an essential requirement for a position. The final two circumstances involve privacy rights in public and private settings.

The role model situation primarily involves clients requiring mental or social rehabilitation. In juvenile detention centers, for example, some patients may have difficulty relating to persons of one sex or the other. In that type of situation, the employer may introduce medical evidence that patient treatment requires the use of same sex employees.

Other "contact" positions may be more difficult
to analyze. The institutional contact setting involves
situations in which the employee comes into visual
or physical contact with clients. This situation will
most likely arise in hospital, prison or nursing home
settings. The basic right involved is the patient's or
inmate's right to privacy.

The watershed case involving prison guards is **Dothard
v. Rawlinson,** 433 U.S. 321 (1977). In **Dothard,** only
males were hired as guards at the Alabama maximum
security prison for men. When challenged, the U.S.
Supreme Court held that female guards would undermine
the security of the prison, and that sex was therefore
a valid BFOQ. The case was limited to this particular
prison setting, however, which was variously described
as having "rampant violence" and a "jungle atmosphere."
The fact that sex offenders were interspersed throughout
the rest of the prison population appeared to influence
a majority of the Court.

In other prison situations, however, courts have
held that women may not be summarily excluded from
contact positions. In many of these cases, the primary
issue is not whether security can be maintained, but
whether the privacy rights of the inmates are being
violated. Most guard situations require body searches
and/or toilet surveillance. When the privacy of the
inmates is at issue, the employer must attempt to
modify job assignments before it may totally exclude
one sex from a particular position. Therefore, if male
guards can be scheduled to supervise activities requiring
male inmate privacy, female guards may not be subject
to total exclusion.

Employers may also be required, in addition to
modifying job assignments, to modify facilities to
insure that privacy interests do not infringe on employment interests. When robes can be distributed, translu-
cent shower screens or other forms of protection in-
stalled, an employer must make the modifications
prior to instituting an employment ban. Economic
defenses to such modifications will not be accepted.
Title VII requires administrative necessity, not merely
inconvenience, to satisfy the BFOQ exception.

Privacy is also the primary concern of contact positions involving sexually segregated establishments in the private sector. The primary example of this situation is a dressing room clerk at a clothing store. Again, if an alternative can be found which protects the privacy interests of the customers, it must be taken. The employer will not be able to meet its burden if the employee can demonstrate that other similar businesses have handled the situation without excluding one sex from employment.

(2) National Origin. In only the narrowest of circumstances will national origin provide a valid BFOQ. Commission Regulation 1606.4 states that a national origin BFOQ will be strictly construed, but provides no examples of when such a BFOQ could be adopted. Except in unique situations such as actors or actresses, the exception would probably not be upheld. While it appears that a role model situation could occur in which a patient requiring mental or social rehabilitation only responds to a certain ethnic group, there are no cases involving this claim to date. In fact, after over 20 years of Title VII protection, there has not been one case determined on national origin BFOQ grounds.

(3) Religion. Although religion can provide an employer with a valid BFOQ, Sections 702 and 703(e) of Title VII provide religious corporations and institutions with direct statutory authority to hire employees of a particular religion. Cases involving religion, therefore, will be analyzed under these statutes because they provide broader protection than the standard BFOQ analysis.

ADEA

As noted above, the casting of actors and actresses provides a prime example of BFOQ. When "The New Leave It To Beaver" television show was being cast, no one was better qualified to play Theodore Cleaver than the original Beaver, Jerry Mathers. Clearly, he was the only individual with experience. The problem, however, is that Jerry Mathers is now too old to portray a child. In fact, absolutely no individual over 40 years of age could reasonably fulfill the requirements of the job.

The law against age discrimination makes an exception for BFOQs. To qualify, an employer must prove that youth is a BFOQ. It may accomplish this in two ways. First, the employer may produce evidence that no individuals over 40 can perform the tasks required. Second, it may show that substantially all older employees could not perform the functions of a job, and that it would be impractical to test each employee on an individual basis.

Prior to January 1986, it would have been difficult to set the parameters for an age BFOQ. Most of the BFOQ cases involved the mandatory retirement of police officers and fire fighters. And, because of the tendency of local forces to allow overweight and out-of-shape younger officers to remain at work, localities had a difficult time explaining why in-shape older workers were being forced out of their jobs.

Congress determined in January 1986, however, that states and cities should be allowed to set the mandatory hiring and retirement ages for fire fighters and law enforcement officers, including jail and prison guards. In 1991, the EEOC is required to propose alternatives, if any are available, to this statutorily approved BFOQ. Until then, however, fire fighters and police officers may be forced into retirement under a bona fide program.

Very few other age BFOQs exist. While physical dexterity and strength often decrease with advanced age, an individual may not be denied employment because of generalizations or stereotypes. Usually, strength and dexterity can be tested. Therefore, while a job may require heavy lifting outside the ability of many older adults, every adult has a right to prove he can successfully perform the job.

This is not to say there are not BFOQs for jobs other than fire fighters and police officers. Prior to 1986, some courts based their BFOQ findings on the fact that a significant number of older individuals suffer from heart disease and that medical science is often unable to accurately detect such disabilities. Also, a Federal Aviation Administration regulation requiring the retirement of commercial pilots at age 60 has been upheld. However, a mandatory retirement age of 65 for school bus drivers was overturned.

From these cases, it appears public safety is a key ingredient to a successful BFOQ defense. However, under most circumstances, the cost of a study to prove the defense would be prohibitive to the employer involved.

Seniority Systems and Benefit Plans

Bona Fide Seniority Systems

(1) Title VII. The statutory defense which affects the greatest number of employees is that which protects bona fide seniority systems under Section 703(h) of Title VII. Seniority systems which determine promotions, wages and layoffs by the length of employment or date of hire do not violate Title VII even if they impact on protected groups within the Act.

Only bona fide seniority systems receive such protection, however. A system is considered bona fide if it was adopted and is maintained without any intent to discriminate against protected groups. Two separate analyses will be conducted, therefore, regarding complaints involving alleged discriminatory seniority systems. The initial analysis will concern whether the layoff or failure to promote was properly instituted under the rules of the seniority policy. The second analysis will involve the historical use of the seniority system as a tool of discrimination.

The most common situation in which seniority is challenged is when the system provides seniority rights exclusively within a bargaining unit or department. Under this system, an employee would forfeit all of his accumulated competitive seniority when transferring into a different department. This type of system, which has the effect of "locking-in" certain employees into lower paying or less desirable departments because of the sacrifice resulting from a transfer, is nevertheless

not a violation of Title VII unless the intent of the
plan was to lock-in minority employees. The fact that
the system actually locks-in a greater percentage
of minority employees does not, in and of itself, strip
a plan of Section 703(h) protection.
Discriminatory intent in this situation is defined
as an actual motive to discriminate. Courts will initially
consider whether a system is applied equally to all
groups. If some white employees, for example, are
allowed to transfer seniority between departments
but black employees are not, the system is not bona
fide. The scrutiny applied to the seniority system will
also come from a historical as well as immediate view-
point. If the seniority system was originally negotiated
to hinder the employment opportunities of minority
applicants, the fact that the program is now maintained
in a neutral manner will not protect its bona fide status.
Specific factors which have led to the removal
of Section 703(h) protection include the failure of
a union to represent all employees, a change in the
terms of the collective bargaining agreement to the
obvious detriment of a minority class and union representatives discouraging minority employees from applying
for certain jobs. A bona fide plan must also be in writing
and applied prior to the employment decision in question.
Employers which originally do not plan to use seniority
in making a promotion decision, but later add that
element to change the selection, will find the decision
to be inherently suspect.
While the racial environment existing at the time
a seniority policy is instituted is of some import, the
fact that a seniority system perpetuates pre-Act discrimination will not, in and of itself, invalidate a system.
The watershed case involving seniority systems, **International Brotherhood of Teamsters v. United States,**
431 U.S. 324, 97 S. Ct. 1843 (1977), held that seniority
systems which were negotiated and maintained free
from illegal purposes would not violate Title VII even
if they impact on certain classes. In **Teamsters,** seniority
accrued only within certain categories of jobs. Therefore, when black employees, who were primarily situated
in less desired departments than white employees

as a result of pre-Act discrimination, attempted to transfer into the more desired departments, they faced a total loss of competitive seniority. Although the U.S. Supreme Court acknowledged the original discrimination by the employer, it found that the union negotiated the collective bargaining agreement and maintained it free of the discriminatory intent. The fact that black employees, on the whole, were adversely affected by the system was not enough to invalidate it.

A plan which shows statistical discrimination, however, will shift the burden of proof onto the employer and union to show that the plan is neutrally applied and furthers the legitimate interests of either the employer or employees. Whether an intra-departmental seniority plan furthers legitimate interests will primarily be determined by the type of industry involved. If the general industry practice is to separate seniority into departments, such a plan will most likely be upheld. A system which eliminates seniority transfers between secretaries and clerks, for example, would not appear to be as rationally structured as a system creating seniority divisions between laborers and office workers. Past National Labor Relations Board decisions will generally provide guidance as to the rationality of a seniority system's structure.

While a seniority system may perpetuate pre-Act discrimination, it is not a license to discriminate. An employee who is successful in an individual claim is presumptively entitled to retroactive seniority to the date he originally should have been hired. Although the rationale behind the seniority exception is to protect valid employee expectations regarding employment, the expectations of beneficiaries of illegal discrimination have not been so protected.

The most recent issue involving seniority is the potential conflict between seniority systems and court ordered affirmative action plans. The problem arises when layoffs are required, which will normally impact on the most recent minority hirees under the affirmative action plan. The U.S. Supreme Court has held that although affirmative action plans are allowed under certain circumstances, the positive goals inherent in such plans do not take priority over bona fide seniority systems. According to the Court, layoffs are too serious a disruption on employees' lives to allow racial goals to supersede seniority rights. Therefore, if layoffs are required, the "last hired-first fired" clause in most seniority agreements must be applied even though a disproportionate number of minority employees will be terminated.

(2) ADEA. As with Title VII, Congress exempted from ADEA coverage bona fide seniority systems. Obviously, this exception has a greater impact on protected classes such as race or sex, since by definition a seniority system provides advantages to employees with greater lengths of service. In fact, any seniority system which gives lesser rights to employees with longer service is not considered bona fide and would violate the Act.

The situation in which a seniority system will most likely give rise to an ADEA claim is when two separate companies merge and their seniority lists must be integrated. The EEOC has stated that it will review such integrations upon the filing of a timely charge. Proof of intent to discriminate is not easily found in that situation, however, because, while one employer's protected age group may suffer a loss of rights, the other company's older employees will benefit.

A seniority system in any circumstance is prohibited from requiring or allowing the involuntary retirement of any individual at least 40 years old because of his age.

The ADEA does not require, however, that a company use seniority as a factor in its employment decisions. Seniority systems may even include additional factors such as merit, capacity or ability. What a seniority system may not consider is the chronological age of the employees. Seniority is measured by length of service and must be uniformly applied to every employee, regardless of age.

The final requirement before a seniority system is considered bona fide under Section 4(f)(2) of the ADEA is the employer must communicate the essential terms and conditions to all of the affected employees. The employer may not create a seniority system to meet its needs after employment determinations are made.

Bona Fide Employee Benefit Plans

In addition to exempting bona fide seniority systems from the ADEA's coverage, Congress exempted bona fide employee benefit plans such as retirement, pension and insurance plans. The purpose of this exemption is to take into account the increased cost to the employer of providing certain benefits to older employees compared to younger employees. An employer may adjust the level of benefits for older employees to the extent necessary to achieve equivalency in employer contributions for older and younger employees. Benefit plans will be considered in compliance with the Act if the actual amount paid or the cost incurred on behalf of an older employee is equal to that for a younger employee. This is true even if the result is a lesser amount of pension or retirement benefits or insurance coverage for the older employee.

The employer seeking to invoke this exemption has the burden of showing that the elements outlined in the Act have been clearly and unmistakably met. The employee benefit plan must be bona fide. A plan is considered bona fide if it has been accurately described in writing to all employees and if the benefits are actually provided in accordance with the plan's written terms. Employees should be notified promptly of the provisions of the plan and any changes so that the employees know how the plan affects them. It is presumed that employees aware of decreasing benefits within a policy will be able to plan accordingly. Also, if the plan clearly prescribes the benefits of a policy, there will be the assurance that the plan will be applied equally to all employees of the same age.

Benefit plans may not be used as a subterfuge to evade the purposes of the ADEA, however. Generally, a decreasing level of benefits must be justified by age-related cost considerations. Valid and reasonable

cost data must be provided, such as data showing that
the actual cost to the employer of providing the particular benefit in question increased over a representative number of years. The employer may rely upon
either cost data compiled on its own employees or
on cost data prepared for a larger group of similarly
situated employees. If reliable data is not available,
the employer must make reasonable projections from
existing data.

(1) Life Insurance. One of the clearest examples
of increased costs coupled with increased age is life
insurance. Life insurance plans may use five-year
age brackets, such as 51-55 or 56-60, for purposes
of analyzing increased cost factors. Therefore, reductions in life insurance benefits for older employees
are permissible provided that the reduction for an
employee of a particular age is no greater than is
justified by the increased cost of coverage for that
employee's specific age bracket.

Example:

Employer X provides $55,000 of life insurance
to employees in age group 41-45. Cost for providing
life insurance to age group 46-50 is ten percent higher.
Employer X may provide age group 46-50 only $50,000
of life insurance since its dollar outlay will be identical
for both groups.

(2) Medical Insurance. An employer may provide
decreased benefits to an older employee if it pays
an equivalent amount in premiums for insuring that
employee. A 1984 amendment precludes an employer
from reducing an employee's coverage by the percentage
covered by Medicare.

(3) Long-Term Disability Plans. Under the Act,
long-term disability benefits may be decreased based
on age-related cost factors. Reductions may be accomplished by reducing the level or duration of the benefits,
or by an appropriate combination of both. For example,
the ADEA would not be violated if, with respect to
disabilities which occur at age 60 or less, benefits

cease at age 65. With respect to disabilities which occur after age 60, an employer could lawfully cease benefits five years after the disablement. Other patterns of reduction supported by employer cost data projections are also legal.

What is not legal are plans which flatly prohibit disability payments after a certain age. While previously the Commission allowed the arbitrary cut-off of disability payments after 70, these benefits must now be available for five years after a disability occurs.

(4) Involuntary Retirement. In 1978, Congress revised the ADEA to address the issue of involuntary retirements and the ADEA's exemption for bona fide seniority systems and bona fide employee benefit plans. Congress' aim was to make it clear that bona fide seniority systems or employee benefit plans may not require or permit the involuntary retirement of an employee within the protected age group based on age. A plan may, however, allow employees to elect early retirement at a specified age at their own option. A plan requiring early retirement for reasons other than age is still allowed under the ADEA.

III.
Theories of Discrimination

DISPARATE TREATMENT

Disparate treatment is when an employer treats one employee differently from another. This treatment can occur in the areas of salaries, promotions, work schedules, pensions, discipline, or any number of other terms or conditions of employment. Whatever the form of the treatment, however, the disparate treatment theory involves the direct comparison of at least two identified employees.

Title VII

Title VII does not require that all employees be treated equally. Title VII requires only that unequal treatment not be the result of factors relating to race, color, religion, sex or national origin. Therefore, the question is not only whether unequal treatment occurred, but whether the employer **intended** the unequal treatment because the employee is a member of a protected group.

Obviously, a claimant under Title VII faces a difficult task. Not only is he required to prove unequal treatment, but he must also become a mind reader and prove the treatment was the result of the discriminatory thoughts of the employer.

In 1973, the United States Supreme Court acknowledged the difficult standard faced by an employee attempting to prove discriminatory intent. In the land-

33

mark case of **McDonnell Douglas v. Green,** 411 U.S. 792 (1973), the Court fashioned a three-step process by which disparate treatment claims are to be analyzed. Employees meeting the evidentiary burdens of each step will have discriminatory intent implied to their situation, even though no direct evidence of an employer's discriminatory intent may exist.

The case of **McDonnell Douglas** involved an individual who was applying for a position. The plaintiff was not hired. In a failure to hire case, the Court stated that an employee must initially show a prima facie case. A prima facie case in a failure to hire situation consists of the following elements: (1) the plaintiff is a member of a protected group; (2) he applied and was qualified for a position; (3) he was denied the position; and (4) the employer continued to seek applicants with similar qualifications.

Once the plaintiff makes out a prima facie case, the burden shifts to the employer to articulate a legitimate non-discriminatory reason for its action. In most cases, the employer's burden is easily met. The employer is not required to prove its case at this stage. It is required only to articulate a defense.

After the employer articulates a non-discriminatory reason, the employee must prove by a preponderance of the evidence that intentional discrimination was a reason for the adverse employment action. The employee can meet this burden by providing facts which show that the employer's articulated reasons are untrue. The employee can also prevail by providing facts which show that discrimination was a determining factor in addition to the employer's articulated reasons. It is not necessary for discrimination to be the sole motivating factor behind an employment decision. It must merely be a determining factor.

Under the **McDonnell Douglas** analysis, the burden of proof always remains with the employee. The employer is not required to prove that discriminatory factors did not play a role. While the employee is required to prove intent, this does not mean willful or deliberate intent. The intent can be subsonscious or subtle. The evidence must show, however, that the unequal treatment was caused by more than chance, inadvertence or mistake. Employees meeting the **McDonnell Douglas** test will have such discriminatory intent inferred.

Prima Facie Case

The **McDonnell Douglas** prima facie case has been modified to a variety of employment situations. The prima facie case for most employment situations will resemble the following: (1) the plaintiff is a member of a protected group; (2) he either is qualified for or is performing a job satisfactorily; (3) he suffers an adverse employment action; and (4) a similarly situated employee who is not a member of the protected group does not suffer the adverse action.

The least difficult requirement to meet is to become a member of a protected group. Everyone is a member of a protected group. Every race, including caucasian, is protected. Males and females are protected. Every employee has a national origin. Title VII, to the surprise of many, does not just protect groups which have suffered historical discrimination. Majority classes are also protected. In addition, combination groups are treated separately. Black females, for example, fall under the protection of Title VII as a distinct group even if the employer does not discriminate against blacks and females as separate groups.

The second element, showing adequate qualifications or job performance, is more problematic. The standard at this stage of the analysis, however, is relatively low. For a current employee, some showing of satisfactory performance is required. This does not mean perfect or even average performance. The employee must merely perform at that level which has been tolerated by the employer in the past.

To the applicant or employee seeking a promotion, a showing of adequate qualifications is required. Again, the standard at this stage is relatively low. The applicant must merely show that he maintains the minimal competency for the position sought. The minimum requirements can be determined by the wording in a newspaper advertisement or a posted job announcement. If the individual actually hired does not possess the advertised qualifications, the qualifications of the employee hired would then set the minimum standards. The third and fourth steps in the prima facie case are met by showing that someone in a similar situation, who is not a member of the plaintiff's protected class, received better treatment from the employer. The definition of similarly situated is made on a case-by-case basis. In a promotion situation, similarly situated employees would include those employees who were considered, or had the qualifications to be considered, for a promotion. In a discipline situation, however, all company employees are similarly situated if all employees are covered by the same company disciplinary policy. Since disparate treatment involves the comparison of individual employees, it is important to identify the specific individuals to be analyzed.

Making out a prima facie case does not mean a plaintiff will win his case. In fact, most employees who file claims with the EEOC will be able to make out a prima facie case. This initial step in the **McDonnell Douglas** theory is primarily used to insure that an employee who files a claim will be able to recover if discrimination is discovered. For example, a law firm which admittedly discriminates against black lawyers would only be liable for claims filed by black lawyers, not all blacks. The prima facie case will inform the judge that this claimant's charge is not frivolous (which, by the way, is also used by many judges to determine whether a claimant is liable for the attorney's fees of the defendant), and that the employee may recover if he proves the intent of the employer was to discriminate.

Employer's Response

Once an employee makes out a prima facie case, the employer must articulate a legitimate non-discriminatory reason for its action. Title VII does not preclude an employer from terminating an employee because of poor performance or a lack of qualifications.

In most situations, the articulated reason will be performance, qualifications or both.

The burden on the employer is a burden of production.
The employer must produce some evidence that it
acted in a non-discriminatory manner. This is compared
to the employee's burden of persuasion. The employee
is required to produce enough evidence that a reasonable
person would be persuaded that discrimination occurred.

The employer is not required to show that its actions
were the correct or fair decisions for a particular
situation. An honestly held but poorly founded decision
is not against the law. The test is not whether the
decision was correct, but whether there was discriminatory animus. An employee fired for suspected theft
will not prevail in his claim merely by proving that
he did not steal company property. He is required
to show that the employer's belief that he stole the
items was based on race, sex or national origin. An
employer's mistakes or arbitrary decisions are only
prohibited if they result from discriminatory motives.

The employer's burden of production does not allow
an employer to use generalizations. Some specificity
in its response is required. For example, an employer
cannot merely argue that it hires the best qualified
applicants, acts in the best interests of the organization
or uses good faith before implementing decisions. It
must produce evidence of how it determined the best
applicants, what it considered in the best interests
of the organization or the type of criteria used in
its good faith decision making.

This does not mean an employer must provide hard
scientific or mathematical evidence. There are two
basic types of evidence which the employer can produce,
objective and subjective. Obviously the employer which
can produce objective evidence—such as attendance,
number of holes drilled or reports written—will have
a much easier time prevailing in the case. There is
no rule, however, against making decisions based on
subjective opinions. The employer that relies on subjective criteria in making employment decisions, however, leaves itself open to challenge.

Sometimes there is no option other than making

a decision based on subjective factors. Non-quantifiable personality conflicts can affect the productivity of an office to the same degree as quantifiable problems. Unless the personality conflict is caused by an employee's race, sex or national origin, the basis for the action is perfectly legal. The problem facing an employer in this situation, however, is convincing the judge that the personal animus is not caused by discriminatory motivations.

Initially, there is a natural skepticism of any opinion which is not easily tested. Making matters worse is when a supervisor or decision maker is of a different race or national origin than the disciplined employee. In this situation, the judge will often infer discriminatory intent. Therefore, an employer that has a good faith subjective rationale for an employment action should document the problem to the greatest extent possible. When the problem involves an employee's poor attitude, the exact words and actions found unacceptable should be documented. Employers which use subjective criteria and maintain statistically unbalanced workforces face an uphill battle under the best circumstances.

Whether based on subjective or objective criteria, the employer's articulated response returns the burden of proof to the employee. In the majority of cases, the third step is required.

Pretext

After the employer has articulated a legitimate non-discriminatory defense, the burden shifts to the employee to prove that the articulated reason is a pretext for discrimination. Pretext means that the employer's rationale is merely a guise or excuse to cover up its true discriminatory motive.

The plaintiff can prove pretext in one of two ways. First, he can show that the employer's rationale is basically unworthy of belief. In the alternative, he can provide evidence that discriminatory factors were more likely the cause, or an additional motivating cause, for the employer's adverse employment action.

To make out a prima facie case, the employee

was required to show that he had minimal competency for the position in question. To prove pretext, however, the employee must show that he has better qualifications than the individual selected. At the very least, the employee must show equal qualifications and some additional evidence of discrimination.

Whether the employee is required to produce additional evidence is made on a case-by-case basis. The issue is whether intent can be inferred strictly from the disparate treatment. In a hiring case, a member of a protected group with better qualifications than the individual selected has sufficient evidence to imply discriminatory intent. Intent can also be inferred in the case of equally qualified individuals if the protected member can show that he applied and was rejected prior to the receipt of the hiree's application. Intent would not be inferred, however, for two equally qualified individuals who apply simultaneously, since Title VII does not require employers to give preference to members of protected groups. In this situation, there is disparate treatment, but without discriminatory statements, statistics or other evidence, there is no proof of discriminatory intent.

Discriminatory intent does not need to be the sole motivating factor behind an adverse employment action. It can be one of many. What is required is for there to be a causal connection between the employee's protected status and the adverse action. Many courts define this connection as "but for." In other words, but for the employee's race, sex, national origin, etc., the employer would have acted differently. Basically, the employee must show his protected status was a significant factor in the employment action.

Exactly how does one challenge an employer's articulated defense? It is imperative that the employee tailor his defense to the employer's response. In many cases, the employee's evidence may show unfairness, but not discrimination. For example, when an employer claims its decisions were based on the employee's last evaluation, it is not enough to show that the employer would have made better decisions had it based its findings on the employee's last five evaluations.

Title VII is not designed to challenge good faith business decisions, correct or incorrect. The employee could challenge the employer's rationale, however, by showing that his last evaluation was tainted by discrimination. Other evidence could be that the employer used only the last evaluation of the protected group employees or the employer's decision to use the last evaluation was because it would eliminate a number of protected class employees.

An employee's claim will also fail if it merely explains the employer's articulated response. An employee terminated for a poor attitude cannot rebut the allegation by explaining that family illnesses or financial pressures precipitated the poor attitude. While arguably management executives should take unexpected hardships into account, Title VII does not guarantee fairness. In this situation, the employee would probably need to argue that non-protected employees were treated more leniently during a crisis or that poor attitudes of non-protected members had not subjected them to termination.

Mere conclusory statements by an employee will not sustain his burden of proof. The fact that an employee perceives that he is performing competently, or is performing better than other employees, is not an issue. The issue is whether the employer's perception of the employee's performance, whether correct or incorrect, was influenced by discriminatory factors. Self-serving statements such as "I was doing a good job," or "I was working twice as hard as a co-worker" are irrelevant without supporting evidence.

There are no guides to the type or amount of evidence required to prove a particular case. Each case must be judged on its own merits. Outside factors such as the judge, demeanor of the witnesses and/or the ability of the attorneys will influence the amount of evidence required. As a rule of thumb, however, the more evidence produced from outside the control of the plaintiff--such as written evaluations, payroll and attendance records, and statements from co-workers--the better the chance of the employee proving his case.

ADEA

The disparate treatment theory under the ADEA is an outgrowth of the Title VII case, **McDonnell Douglas**, discussed above. Under **McDonnell Douglas**, a plaintiff is required initially to prove his prima facie case. In ADEA terms, a prima facie case consists of showing: (1) the employee is 40 years of age or older; (2) the employee was the victim of an adverse employment action such as discharge, demotion or failure to be hired or promoted; (3) the employee was qualified for the position; and (4) the employee has evidence that age was a factor in the decision. In the majority of cases, the fourth requirement will be met by showing that an employee was replaced by a younger worker. While the younger employee does not necessarily have to be under 40 years of age, the wider the disparity in ages between the employees in question, the greater the inference that age played a role in the decision.

As discussed under Title VII, once an employee establishes a prima facie case, the burden shifts to the employer to articulate a legitimate non-discriminatory reason for the adverse employment action taken against the older employee. The word "articulate" means just that. The employer need only produce, not prove, some evidence which explains its action. In most cases, the employer will allege that the younger employee was either more qualified or productive than the older employee.

After the employer has articulated a legitimate defense, the burden shifts back to the employee to prove that the employer's reason was not the real reason he was demoted or discharged. The ultimate burden is on the employee to prove his case. Using sports terminology, a tie goes to the employer. Although the burden is on the employee, it is not an extremely difficult burden to meet. The employee need only prove his case by a preponderance of the evidence. That is, the employee's side of the story need only be slightly more believable than the employer's side. He is not required to prove his case beyond a reasonable doubt, as would a prosecutor in a criminal trial.

One court has simplified the sequence of proof into one simple question—did the employee produce sufficient evidence to permit a reasonable factfinder to conclude that age was a determining factor in the employer's decision?

There are a number of avenues by which an employee can attempt to prove his case. There is direct evidence ("Jane, I'm firing you because you are too old"), circumstantial evidence (Jane was fired even though her job evaluations were better than her younger counterparts') or statistical evidence (Jane and all other employees over 40 were fired).

While a detailed analysis of the types of evidence which have proven successful and unsuccessful at trial is provided below, it is important to understand that the employee must prove that age was a "but for" cause of an adverse employment action. In other words, but for an employee's age, an action would not have been taken. It is not enough, although it can be helpful to a case, to prove that the employer was unfair to an employee or that the employer made a bad business decision. If an employer can show that an older job applicant was not hired because he wore a red tie to an interview, and the employer proves that it never hires anyone who wears red ties, the employer would be successful regardless of the unfairness of its decision. Obviously, an employer would never use this defense, for even if true, a jury would find it implausible. However, the point to be emphasized is that the ADEA was not created to second guess legitimate business decisions made by an employer. The Act only protects against decisions influenced by the age of the employees, and the court will so instruct the jury.

While examining the types of evidence most frequently used to prove disparate treatment, it is important to note that no formula exists which can accurately predict the outcome of a trial. Many factors beyond the evidence presented are involved. For example, a jury can be either plaintiff or defendant oriented. In addition, the judge has some discretion as to the type of evidence which he will allow the jury to hear. Last, but certainly not least, is the plaintiff himself.

The plaintiff's ability to present his side of the story in a sympathetic light is the most important element to a plaintiff's lawsuit. In many instances, there are no witnesses to contested conversations other than the employee and the manager. It is the jury's job to decide whom to believe. Often, the only way for a jury to decide who is telling the truth is by considering the demeanor of the person testifying. No matter what the evidence or situation presented, there is no more important element than the individual claiming he was wronged.

Evidence of Disparate Treatment

Evidence is found in many shapes and sizes. The weight afforded each type of evidence can only be determined on a case-by-case basis in the context of the employment situation involved. The following types of frequently alleged evidence, therefore, are inclusive and not exclusive ways of proving a case of discrimination.

Evaluations

If man's best friend is a dog, the employee's best friend is a strong evaluation. People can and will say almost anything in a courtroom; judges and jurors are well aware of this. Written evaluations do not change, however, despite the passage of time.

The plaintiff is the first to put on his case at trial. If a plaintiff can present a series of evaluations prepared by his opponent, lauding his performance, the defendant will be hard pressed to rebut this evidence with mere words to the contrary.

One mistake a plaintiff often makes, however, is failing to listen to the employer's rationale behind a discharge. Especially when a new management team or philosophy is introduced, an employee's ability to adapt may be weighed more heavily than other categories of an evaluation. An overall good evaluation, with low marks for creativity, is not likely to overcome a defense that a company is emphasizing new techniques.

Generally, however, an employee with outstanding evaluations cannot be defeated by words alone. The subjective testimony of a plaintiff or defendant is almost always defeated by evaluations or reviews which state the contrary.

A second scenario is the employee with a history of good evaluations, but a poor evaluation just prior to being demoted or discharged. An employee has at least two defenses to an unsatisfactory evaluation. The first involves timing. When an employee's evaluation scores drop immediately before an adverse action, the employer will be required to explain the legitimacy of the review, that is, how an employee's ratings could plummet from excellent to unsatisfactory in a short period of time. While this actually may have occurred, it is usually viewed as unlikely without corresponding objective evidence. Second, if an employee can prove that his performance remained constant, but evaluations fluctuated, the employer will face an almost impossible task of explaining the validity of the criteria used to judge the employee. This task is particularly difficult if the same person judged each evaluation.

On the other hand, a claimant who receives numerous mediocre reviews will likely be unsuccessful by simply arguing about the fairness of the reviews. The Acts were not intended to challenge business determinations, whether correct or incorrect, if race, sex, national origin or age did not influence the decision. An employee who signs his evaluations without making any comment on them may be precluded from disputing the validity of those evaluations. In such an instance, the employee's best possible claim is that the mediocre marks were still equal or better than those of an employee outside a protected class who was treated differently.

When judging the fairness of an employee's evaluation, the court will focus on the criteria used. The evaluation should primarily be based on the quality or quantity of work. The more specific the criteria, the more particulars of performance, the stronger the evidence.

Prior Discriminatory Acts

At times, an employee will seek to introduce into evidence the past discriminatory acts of an employer. The employer, on the other hand, may want to offer evidence of instances when it hired or promoted other employees within the protected class. In both cases, the litigants hope that jurors will believe that they are acting in a similar fashion today.

A court will admit evidence of prior acts, good or bad, if the evidence is relevant. Evidence is relevant if it will help with the determination of the case at hand. The testimony of a similarly situated co-worker terminated at the same time as the plaintiff will likely shed light on whether the employer had discriminatory intentions at the time of the discharges. Evidence of discrimination five years prior to the act in question, however, would probably not be relevant unless it occurred under identical circumstances and involving identical parties.

Over 95 percent of the cases which the EEOC litigates result in settlements prior to decision. These settlements rarely will be admissible in another trial, however. The settlements themselves usually state that no finding of fault has been made and that parties will not use the terms of the settlement in other court actions. To encourage employers to settle, courts generally will not admit such settlements. Court judgements are much more likely to be admitted.

What the courts will not do, however, is try the case of a witness. If the witness has first-hand knowledge about the plaintiff's case, or if the witness' situation is closely related to the plaintiff's claim, the evidence may be relevant. The court will have no interest, however, in trying a witness' charge of discrimination.

What is most important is the complaining employee's work history. Events which occurred prior to the statute of limitations, such as a demotion years back, still may be relevant to a present termination case. While damages cannot be recovered for the untimely demotion claim, the facts behind the demotion might shed light on the timely filed termination charge.

Timing of Disciplinary Actions

Proof of a dischargeable offense usually precludes a plaintiff from successfully maintaining a discrimination action. The timing of a discharge, however, may invite questions as to whether the offense was the real reason behind the termination. When an act leading to discipline comes months or years prior to the adverse employment action, it gives the appearance that the employer merely manufactured a defense when faced with a discrimination charge. Questions requiring answers are:

(1) Who knew about the bad act? If the individual making the final termination decision previously knew of the offense but took no action, the implication is that the offense was not considered critical. However, the fact that a supervisor took no action, but was later overruled by his superior after the superior became aware of the act, would likely defeat a discrimination claim.

(2) Was the employee confronted about his action? Dischargeable offenses usually are grounds for immediate confrontation. An employer which has knowledge of a violation of company policy but never discusses the violation with the employee tacitly approves the conduct. It is especially difficult for an employer to claim an employee's act affected his performance, if the employer fails to mention such act on an employee's evaluation.

(3) How much time has passed between an employee's bad act and his discipline? A day, a week, a year, three years? Obviously, the longer a company waits to discipline an employee, the greater the inference that its reason is a pretext for discrimination.

(4) Was the employee replaced by another employee? While an action may not normally create a reason to fire an employee, it may be relevant for an employer which is attempting to reduce its workforce. For example, in deciding whether to retain either of two employees, a dischargeable offense not previously disciplined may nevertheless make the difference in who is selected.

Position Titles

During company reductions-in-force or reorganizations, new titles or designations are often created for retained employees. An associate manager, for example, may have his title changed to assistant director. In an ADEA action, the fact that a younger employee is not passed the precise title of a discharged older employee does not preclude the older employee from prevailing in his case. In such a situation, he need only show that a majority or substantial number of his previous job duties have been reassigned to the younger worker.

In a situation involving merged positions, the plaintiff must be able to show that he has the ability to satisfactorily perform all the duties of the new job. While past evaluations may show that an employee successfully handled his old responsibilities, they may not show that he could successfully carry out new ones. Only under the most egregious circumstances, such as having an employer admit it merged two positions for the purpose of terminating an older employee, will the EEOC or courts question a business determination to reduce the number of personnel.

Warnings

Exacerbating the trauma of being terminated, many employees complain about the fact that they were provided absolutely no warning prior to their dismissal. After years of loyal service, one day they are called into the boss' office and told to pack their belongings. Fair? Usually not. Proof of discrimination? Again, usually not.

The fact is the amount of warning, or lack thereof, is usually irrelevant to the proffered reasons for an employee's discharge. There are no pain and suffering damages under the Acts, so the pain felt by the employee is not an issue.

When the lack of warning is most relevant, however, is when the employer maintains a policy of progressive discipline requiring a warning. Anytime an employer

fails to follow its own standards, such as a written
warning for the first offense, three-day suspension
for the second offense and discharge for the third
offense, there is an inference of discrimination. Failing
an employer's policy requiring written warnings prior
to discharge, however, the lack of warnings is not
relevant.

Disparaging Statements

Disparaging statements about an employee are
a common form of evidence in discrimination complaints.
In racial, national origin and sexual harassment cases,
which are analyzed in greater detail in following sections, the type and frequency of the statements are
of particular importance. Whether a particular statement
is deemed offensive is typically easier to determine
in race, sex or national origin contexts. What often
proves more complex are statements which may or
may not represent an age-related animus.

In most age-related charges, it is alleged that someone from management told the terminated party that
age played a role in the discharge. Either before, during
or after the termination, it is alleged someone mentioned
something related to age. Not surprisingly, in a majority
of these cases, the manager who allegedly made the
comments cannot remember saying them. Just as
predictably, there are no witnesses to the alleged
conversations other than the parties involved.

In such a situation, who can be believed? And even
if the older employee is believed, does it have any
significance? Unfortunately, there are no formulas
to judge the effects of statements on particular juries.
There are, however, trends on the types of statements
and particular situations in which such evidence proves
most successful.

Clearly, age-related statements can be used as
circumstantial evidence to prove the intent of an employer to discriminate. The first step is to identify
the relationship between the individual making the
statement and the employee.

In termination cases, age statements will be relevant

if they are made by the terminating officer. The fact that co-workers, or equals, joke with an individual about his age does not show that age played a factor in the employer's decision. Likewise, a statement by a personnel director who signs the discharge paper, but has no first-hand knowledge of the circumstances behind the decision, would not be imputed to the intent of the employer. The statements must be shown to have come from someone directly responsible for the employment decision.

One exception to the decision maker rule is when the decision maker's supervisor is shown to have made age-related comments which were or could have been overheard by his subordinates. It can be inferred in such situations that subordinate managers would be affected, in a sense instructed, to use age in their decisions. It is important to produce evidence that the subordinates heard such comments, however, since in many circumstances the managers will deny hearing the statements or understanding them.

Once a statement is identified as being made by the decision maker, the statement must be placed in context. The statement that an employee is "not as young as he used to be" would obviously show greater discriminatory intent if made during a board meeting than a softball game or at the company picnic. Certainly, the statement should have some connection to the employee's performance rather than a social or non-performance situation.

As explained earlier, statements are often alleged to have been made in conversations with no witnesses. Corroboration is extremely helpful. Obviously, testimony from a party without an interest in a case carries much greater weight than from an individual whose livelihood may be at stake. At the very least, an employee should make a notation at the earliest possible moment which states the time, date and setting of a discriminatory statement. Although the notation is not admissible as evidence, jurors may be positively influenced by a witness' ability to remember details.

It is impossible to list the phrases which win and lose cases. The term "bright young people" will carry great weight if combined with a large amount of other evidence, but will probably carry no weight when standing as the only evidence of age discrimination. However, it is important to analyze the ambiguity inherent in certain phrases. Phrases such as "set in his ways," "dead wood" or the desire to "clean house" can have both discriminatory and non-discriminatory meanings. By definition, they could describe young or old employees. Statements such as "over-aged and overpaid," "pensionable" or "60 is really getting up there" clearly refer to age. An employer that mentions the employee's exact age, without an apparent reason for knowing it, might show an intent to use such knowledge in a discriminatory action. While age-related comments can help a case, it is rarely advisable to rely on the statements alone. Usually the weight provided the statements will be no greater or less than the strength of the rest of a case.

Knowledge of an Employee's Age

While it is not technically improper for an employer to ask an applicant his age during an interview, such questioning can be used as evidence of discrimination in a failure-to-hire case. This mistake is rarely made, however, in an era of greater awareness of protection against age discrimination.

More prevalent are employers which list employee ages on forms used in making reduction-in-force decisions. A company memorandum requesting a list of the ages of employees, even when used in conjunction with other information, can be extremely damaging to an employer's defense. Ages compiled on old forms or by inadvertence, however, are more problematic for the employee. In this situation, the employee would probably be required to show that the ages were used or compiled at some time near the date of the alleged discriminatory act.

DISPARATE IMPACT

In certain circumstances, gross statistical disparities can, in and of themselves, constitute a violation of Title VII or the ADEA. Unlike the disparate treatment theory, disparate impact requires no proof of intentional discrimination. The fact that a class of employees is injured by an employer's policy automatically shifts the burden to the employer to show that the policy is required by business necessity.

Title VII

The landmark case establishing the disparate impact theory is **Griggs v. Duke Power Co.**, 401 U.S. 424, 91 S. Ct. 849 (1971). The **Griggs** case involved a North Carolina company which required entry–level labor applicants to possess a high school diploma and pass a general intelligence test. Census statistics at the time showed that while approximately 34 percent of white males had high school diplomas, only 12 percent of black males had graduated. The impact of the intelligence test was even greater, with 58 percent of white males passing the test and only six percent of blacks. The company's requirements therefore significantly impacted on the number of blacks hired.

The tests were applied to both blacks and whites in a neutral fashion. Any individual, whether white or black, who did not pass the company's requirements was disqualified. Despite the fact that the Court found no intent to use the tests in a discriminatory fashion, the Court majority held that the impact itself was an illegal barrier to an employment opportunity.

Title VII does not guarantee a job to every person regardless of qualifications. Nor does it guarantee special privileges for minority groups. What the disparate impact theory prohibits is artificial barriers to minority hiring. When an employer's policy or practice does impede minority hiring, the employer is required to show that its policy or practice is necessary to the safe and efficient operation of the business.

Safe and efficient operation is generally defined as "business necessity." In other words, the employer must show that the policies it uses to make business decisions, if impeding upon the lawful right of a minority to be considered for employment, must actually be related to job performance. In the **Griggs** case, employees without high school diplomas had historically performed as well as high school graduates. The Court, therefore, found there was no business necessity to the employer's requirement.

Under disparate treatment, an employer's good faith action, even if mistaken, vindicates the employer. Under disparate impact, however, the employer is not allowed to be mistaken. If the policy does not improve the operation of the business, a violation occurs. In fact, not only must the policy increase work efficiency, the employer must be able to show that it increases efficiency.

Even if the employer can show that its neutrally applied policy is job related, the employees in the impacted group have a final opportunity to show that an alternative policy is available. The alternative must have less impact and also protect the employer's interest in upgrading job performance. If two or more alternatives are available, the employer must use the policy with the least impact.

Unfortunately, mathematically proving that an alternative policy actually protects an employer's interest is an expensive proposition. In fact, it is usually an expensive proposition for an employer to show that its test or policies are business related.

For plaintiffs with the money and patience, however, the disparate impact theory offers an opportunity through statistics to shift the burden to the employer.

Adverse Impact

The inquiry under disparate impact is into consequences and not motive. The employee must establish that an employment practice, although applied equally to all applicants or employees, has the effect of excluding a significant number of women or minority groups.

The first step is identifying the neutral policy or practice which excludes a large number of applicants from employment. In **Griggs**, the policy was the requirement of a high school diploma and passing an intelligence test. Other policies might include a no-spouse rule in a company primarily staffed by males; word-of-mouth job recruitment when the workforce is primarily white; or the failure to consider job experience over five years, which would impact on older employees under the ADEA. In most instances, however, the employer will require a test which one minority group or other fails to pass in equal percentages as a majority group.

Usually the policy will include an objective factor, which can be graded or tested. Sometimes it will involve an unfavorable quality, such as a criminal record, in which an employer automatically excludes an applicant from consideration. (The EEOC has held that the exclusive use of criminal records in hiring decisions impacts against blacks.) In the recent past, when the employee was unable to identify a neutral policy or practice leading to the adverse employment action, the case was analyzed under the disparate treatment theory, that is, the reason the employer failed to judge one individual under the same criteria as another. More cases involving subjective criteria which impact against minorities will certainly be heard in the future, however, as a result of the 1988 Supreme Court decision in **Watson v. Fort Worth Bank and Trust**, 108 S. Ct. 2777 (1988). In that case, the Court held that a black bank teller denied a promotion based on her supervisors' subjective recommendations could use statistics which showed that white employees were four times more likely to be selected for promotion. (See Pattern and Practice below.)

If the analysis is under disparate impact, however, the policy must concern an employer's standard operating procedure. Impact theory is unavailable for random or sporadic acts. If unusual circumstances affect a company, such as a wildcat strike, the case would likely be analyzed under disparate treatment. Likewise, when the employer has a policy which would impact on a group if enforced, but the policy actually is enforced sporadically, the case again would be analyzed under disparate treatment. The issue in this situation is the reason the policy was enforced, when under normal circumstances it is not. A policy which is not enforced is really no policy at all.

If a policy or practice can be specifically defined, the next question is whether it impacts on a protected group. This is accomplished by comparing the percentage of applicants selected from a minority group against the percentage of applicants selected from the majority group.

Emphasis should be placed on the word applicant. Unless the employer has a policy which discourages members of a protected group from applying for positions, the statistical analysis will focus on the **percentage** of minority group and majority group members passing a particular test. There is no impact claim from the mere showing of more males than females or significantly more whites than blacks. An allegation involving a position requiring unique qualifications must be based on statistics which focus on employees possessing those unique qualifications. General population statistics are relevant to unskilled, not skilled, positions.

A word of warning to employees seeking positions requiring unique qualifications. There may be insufficient numbers of employees from which a statistical analysis can be made. In most circumstances, a pool of thirty or fewer applicants will not prove statistically significant, although statistics involving a small sample size may still provide evidence under disparate treatment analysis. The fact that a statistic may look suspect to an average individual does not mean that the statistic will be significant under the scrutiny of a professional.

While statistics cannot be based on a sample size which is too small by necessity, the employee is also not allowed to restrict the sample size by desire. For example, an employee who can show the impact of a test when considering employees within one division or department, but cannot show impact when results are compiled from throughout the company, is not allowed to restrict the analysis to his division. As a rule, statistical accuracy improves with sample size. Therefore, statistics should be based upon the greatest number of individuals reasonably possessing the characteristics of the applicant pool.

An expert can advise an individual whether there are enough employees on which to base a statistical opinion. The expert may have a more difficult time determining whether the disparate impact itself is significant. Just having a disproportional effect to prove a violation has been variously described as substantial, significant or marked. In layman's terms, statistics must not only raise one's curiosity, they must convince a reasonable person that there is almost no possibility that the results came about by chance.

Statistical probability is most often based on "standard deviations." The standard deviation theory was accepted by the United States Supreme Court in **Hazelwood Indep. School Dist. v. United States**, 433 U.S. 299, 97 S. Ct. 2736 (1977). In **Hazelwood**, the Court stated that a standard deviation of less than three, which equates to a five percent probability of occurring by chance, would probably not meet the impact burden without additional evidence. Statistical disparities of greater than three deviations, however, will usually support an impact claim. The Court made clear, however, that raw statistics alone should not control the judicial decision. Other evidence, such as direct evidence of discrimination for example, would lessen the statistical burden. A company with a good track record regarding minority employment could have the plaintiff's statistical burden increased.

Space does not allow a detailed explanation for deriving a standard deviation. The EEOC enacted Regulation 1607.4, called the 4/5's rule, as a general guide. A test or policy which selects any minority group at an 80 percent rate or less when compared to the majority group selection rate is suspect. The EEOC will then conduct further statistical analysis to confirm or refute the possible disparate impact.

One issue often arising is when just one portion of a test impacts against a minority group, but the test as a whole does not. Many employers have used this "bottom-line" justification with mixed results. Although this issue of law is still under development, it appears the bottom-line defense is most successful when the portion of the test in question does not constitute an absolute barrier to employment. For example, if a fire fighter test requires an applicant to lift 100 pounds, the test would likely impact on females. Unless the employer can show that lifting 100 pounds is a minimum requirement for the position, and not just show that strength is a desired quality, an absolute requirement that an applicant lift this weight would violate Title VII. If strength is just one portion of a test which measures all of the requirements necessary for a fire fighter, however, and the test as a whole does not impact on females, the weight lifting requirement would probably be allowed. The EEOC Guidelines state that the Commission does not require each facet of a test to be non-discriminatory if the test as a whole is non-discriminatory.

Nothing in Title VII precludes the use of tests or measuring procedures. When the tests or measuring procedures impact on a protected group, however, the employer must be able to prove that their use has produced a more efficient workforce.

Business Necessity

Once disparate impact has been proven, the employer is required to justify the policy by showing that it is related to business necessity. In order to establish business necessity, the employer must provide evidence that a relationship exists between its selection procedure and performance on the job. This is typically accomplished through the use of validity studies.

Because the policy behind Title VII is to open employment opportunities, courts will closely scrutinize employment policies with proven impact. Unlike disparate treatment, in which an employer will be successful if it can prove a good faith belief that its policy works, the employer under the impact theory must have statistics which prove that its policy works.

As with standard deviations, detailed explanations

of validity studies and their components are best left to the experts. Generally, however, there are three different strategies to validate a test: criterion-related validation, content validation and construct validation. In reality, only the first two are actually used.

Content validation is typically the easiest to show. Content validation is when the test closely resembles the job in question, such as a typing test for a secretary or an editing test for a copy editor. The test actually measures the critical work behavior required in a position. Content validity does not measure mental processes, such as intelligence, personality or leadership. If these are important factors for a position, and the employer wishes to test applicants on these factors, the employer must prepare a more difficult and expensive criterion-related validity study.

Discriminatory tests are impermissible unless shown, by professionally accepted methods, to be predictive of or significantly correlated with important elements of work behavior which comprise the job for which candidates are being evaluated. When the trait required in a position is intelligence, an employer may give each applicant a test which the employer believes measures intelligence. If the test impacts on a minority group, however, the test must be criterion validated.

A test is criterion validated when test scores are compared to job performance. Basically, the employer will provide statistics, through a professional, which show that its best employees graded highest on the test and its worst employees graded lowest. In the **Griggs** case, employees without a high school diploma performed as well as employees with a high school diploma. Therefore, when the company instituted its high school diploma requirement, it could not pass a criterion-related validity test.

A company which believes its tests are criterion valid must have the paperwork to prove it. One of the basic tenets in the EEOC's Uniform Guidelines On Employee Selection Procedures is that employer's tests should be in written form, from the instructions given the expert to the expert's final findings. By requiring written studies, the EEOC protects its rights and the rights of private litigants to challenge a report's accuracy.

Obviously, validating a test can prove expensive. Under EEOC Guidelines, tests must be professionally developed. Some employers may be able to validate their tests by using studies conducted by other companies in the same area or field. This is only allowed, however, when there are no significant differences between the studied and unstudied jobs. Even if the skills are the same, the responsibilities may be different. For employers without studies to borrow, there are few shortcuts. Although a company is not required to follow the Commission Guidelines defining the standards for validation, courts have given the Guidelines great deference. The employer who fails to follow the Guidelines will generally bear a heavy burden, and generally fail, in proving job relatedness.

Alternative Tests

Once an employer shows that its tests are job related, the employee still has an opportunity to show that an alternative test is available which protects the employer's interests and has less impact on the minority group. Realistically, the employee is at a severe disadvantage at this stage of a proceeding. An employee's best argument will almost always involve the previous issue of job relatedness.

If the employee finds himself in this situation, however, the most likely alternative will involve some variation on the employer's validated study. Even if an employer can show that its tests and procedures accurately predict successful job performance, the accuracy of a test might not be as finely tuned as the employer argues. While there may be statistical proof that an employee scoring 90 on a test performs better on the job than an employee scoring 70, there may be no proof that a person scoring 91 will perform better than someone scoring 90. If grouping the test scores in five point categories or more will protect the employer's interests, and also result in less impact, the employer can be forced to group the applicants.

The plaintiff must be able to prove that there will be less impact and that the employer's interests will be protected. Just as the employer is forced to jump through the validation hoops, the plaintiff must validate its alternatives. Mere articulation of other possible test methods for employees will not meet its burden.

ADEA

The disparate impact theory under the ADEA is based upon the same theory as spelled out in **Griggs v. Duke Power Co.** under Title VII. This theory applies when the employer's adverse employment action is not based on an intent to discriminate, but results from a facially neutral policy which affects a significantly greater number of older than younger employees.

The requirements for a successful impact claim have been thoroughly discussed in the Title VII section. Under the ADEA, an employee must initially show that a facially neutral policy has a disparate impact on a protected age group. One example of a facially neutral policy is a rule prohibiting the hiring of anyone with over ten years of experience in a field. This policy could technically prevent the hiring of an individual 30 years of age as well as applicants over 50. The effect, however, would have a much greater impact on individuals in the over-40 protected age group, however, since they typically have worked for a greater number of years. Although facially neutral, the impact is felt by older employees.

Other policies which are facially neutral but could impact on older employees include the refusal to hire individuals over a certain salary or educational level, terminating employees in exclusively higher paying job categories during a reduction in force, or refusing to consider experience acquired over ten years from the date of application.

A primary requirement of disparate impact cases is that there actually be disparate impact. Although seemingly redundant, the failure of statistics to show significant disparate impact has proven the death knell of many claims. A policy which changes the aver-

age age of employees from 35 to 33 is not sufficient.
Exactly where the line between impact and non-impact
falls is difficult to state. However, most courts and
the EEOC require at least a 20 percent greater impact
on one age group when compared to another. An adverse
effect on a single employee, or even a few employees,
is not sufficient.

Another difficult issue involves identifying the
group of employees who are impacted by a policy. For
example, a protected employee who can show that
he was not hired because of an employer's policy not
to consider experience over five years in the past
apparently will make out a prima facie case. If by
pure chance, however, the employer proves that it
still hired the same percentage of older employees
that one would expect from the local applicant labor
pool, the employer may have a valid defense. In other
words, the employer may have another policy which
discriminates against younger workers so that it all
evens out in the end. The EEOC would argue that if
the first practice discriminates against older employees,
there is a violation of the ADEA. The EEOC's own
regulations, however, allow it to consider an employer's
total equal employment status when considering the
impact of a policy. The courts appear split on the
issue. Until finally resolved, it would be helpful to
show that a disproportionate workforce actually exists.

Once an employee has shown disparate impact,
he is not required to prove that the employer's intent
in establishing the policy was to discriminate against
older employees. Once impact is shown, the burden
shifts to the employer to show that the policy is job-related. A classic example of job relatedness under
the ADEA involves older employees and fitness tests.
Obviously, many fitness tests impact on older age
groups. A fitness test for a lifeguard position would
be job-related, however, while a fitness test for an
accountant's position would not.

A detailed explanation of the specific analysis
required to prove a disparate impact case is provided
under Title VII. Individuals should be aware, however,
that impact studies are usually expensive to conduct.

Most age claimants will have to rely on EEOC experts because of the financial expenditures involved.

Pattern and Practice

Pattern and practice analysis is very similar to that used in disparate impact cases. Both theories rely heavily on statistics, although pattern and practice cases usually include some additional evidence of discrimination. When statistics alone do not prove adverse impact, a pattern and practice case can still be built by buttressing those statistics with other types of evidence, such as discriminatory statements from the employer. When examined together, statistics and direct evidence may show that the employer engaged in a pattern and practice of discrimination when making employment decisions.

The importance of proving a pattern and practice of discrimination is shifting the burden of proof. In most cases, an employee is required to prove that he was the victim of discrimination. Employers that are found to have engaged in a pattern of discrimination, however, must prove that they did not discriminate against minority employees. Courts infer that all members of the class are victims of discrimination.

Pattern and practice cases may involve both objective and subjective employment devices. Although pattern and practice cases do not need the statistically significant numbers of employees required to prove impact cases, the evidence must show that discrimination was a standard operating procedure of a company. Two or three isolated incidents of minority employees failing to be promoted will not be considered a pattern and practice.

Pattern and practice cases of greater magnitude, however, recently received a boost from the United States Supreme Court. In **Watson v. Fort Worth Bank and Trust,** 108 S. Ct. 2777 (1988), the Court held that subjective promotion devices, such as interviews and supervisory opinions, are subject to the same disparate analysis as used in impact cases. Impact cases normally involve an identifiable test which burdens one group more heavily than another. In **Watson,** a variety of reasons were used by the employer for its failure to promote minority employees. Although there was not one specific policy causing a disparity, the Court ruled that statistics could still be used to show that black applicants were four times less likely to receive a promotion than white applicants.

IV.
Current Issues in Employment Law

RACE DISCRIMINATION

The majority of race discrimination complaints will fall under the disparate treatment analysis discussed in an earlier chapter. Unique options and analyses are created by certain race and national origin complaints, however, which are the subject of this chapter. Although race and national origin are separate classes under Title VII, they are interchangeable for purposes of the following subjects.

Racial Harassment

A major branch of case law has developed regarding employers which subject their minority employees to hostile working conditions on a plant-wide or company-wide basis. Title VII does not just protect the wage and promotional opportunities of employees, but also working conditions which impact on one's self dignity. Title VII is violated when employees are subjected to hostilities because of their race. These hostilities may take the form of words, graffiti or physical incidents.

The primary issue is when a racial slur creates a racially hostile atmosphere. A racially hostile environment is not created by an isolated incident of racial intolerance. The fact that an employee tells an isolated racial joke will not meet the standard for creating a racially hostile atmosphere. Hostile atmospheres

63

are created by a series or pattern of such occurrences. Likewise, one note or racially motivated memorandum will not meet the standard unless it is reproduced and widely distributed. Whether the number of incidents creates a hostile work environment is determined on a case-by-case basis, including such factors as the nature of the acts or words, the frequency of the encounters, the total number of days in which the offensive acts occur and the context of the offensive conduct. The number of insensitive jokes tolerated on an oil rig, for example, would be greater than that tolerated in a white-collar office setting.

Employees who prove that they are victims of racial insensitivity on a daily or weekly basis will meet the required standard. The indignities may focus on one employee or an entire class of employees of a certain race. The fact that the intended object of racial slurs may have been one particular individual will not protect an employer from charges by other employees. In fact, it has been held that a white employee may sue because of a hostile environment afflicting black employees. Racially hostile environments are disturbing to all races.

The fact that an employee can prove he suffered from or witnessed repeated episodes of racial harassment from fellow employees does not create, in and of itself, liability for the employer, however. To violate Title VII, an employer must have known or should have known that such activity was occurring. This may be proven in one of two ways. First, an employee can complain of the acts to management, thereby providing the employer with direct knowledge. Second, the acts can be so pervasive or prolonged that the employer is considered to have constructive knowledge of their occurrence. An employer that is not made aware of racially hostile acts, however, cannot be found liable for condoning or tolerating the offensive incidents.

An employer that is aware of racial harassment may still avoid liability by taking immediate and appropriate corrective actions. Unless the acts are perpetrated by high management officials, whose actions would be considered synonymous with the company, employers which swiftly and decisively correct such problems will not be held responsible for the acts of non-management employees. From that point on, however, the employer must prevent further occurrences. Employees alleging racial harassment are subject to the same standards as the employer. Employees who participate in racially motivated incidents may not later complain that those incidents affected their work environment. The fact that an employee uses vulgar language, however, is not consent for other employees to use racially derogatory language. A case in which a white woman remained in a relationship with a black man, even after he beat her, did not provide consent for other employees to harass her through the use of racially derogatory language.

An employer which maintains a hostile work environment will be forced to correct it. For an employee who is terminated, proving a racially hostile environment will shift the burden of persuasion to the employer to show that the employee was discharged for non-discriminatory reasons. While an employee with a poor attendance or work record may still be unsuccessful in winning his case, an employee often can show that the employer's hostile environment detracted from his performance. An employer is not allowed to discipline an employee for natural responses to conditions found in a hostile work environment.

42 U.S.C. Sections 1981 and 1983

In race cases, claimants should be aware that the statutes above may be used in conjunction with, or separate from, a Title VII claim. Although Sections 1981 and 1983 were adopted shortly after the Civil War to protect the rights of black citizens, they have recently been used by Arabs, Jews and other non-white individuals. White individuals also may use these statutes if they encounter discrimination because of their inter-action with or assistance to non-white individuals. These statutes do not protect citizens against discrimination based on sex or religion, however. (Jews are considered a race under these statutes.)

The statutes have strengths and weaknesses. A basic strength includes the fact that compensatory and punitive damages are possible to a prevailing party, which are not allowed under Title VII. A second improvement over Title VII is the fact that the claim can be heard by a jury, which often is more sympathetic than a judge.

The most glaring weakness when compared to Title VII is the fact the plaintiff must litigate these claims on his own behalf. The EEOC does not have jurisdiction under these statutes and cannot enforce a client's rights. In fact, the EEOC will not advise clients, other than to make them aware of the statutes, of the advisability of bringing such a claim.

As to the statutes themselves, Section 1981 provides all persons with the right to make and enforce contracts as is enjoyed by white citizens. Courts have held that employment situations involve actual or implied contracts between the employer and employee, therefore bringing Section 1981 into disputes involving hirings, terminations and promotions. Section 1983, on the other hand, basically reaches counties and municipalities that encroach on rights protected by Section 1981.

Section 1981 claims are analyzed under the same standards as set in Title VII. The **McDonnell Douglas** disparate treatment model will be the primary form of analyzing claims under this section. Unlike Title VII, Section 1981 requires proof of an employer's intent to discriminate. The fact that an employer's policies may impact on a protected group is not sufficient to violate Section 1981. While Section 1983 does not have a specific intent requirement, the intent to violate an individual's rights will probably come from the constitutional or statutory violation which is required by the statute. As a rule, evil motive is required.

An important use of Section 1981 is for statute of limitations purposes. In most circumstances, an employee who fails to file his Title VII claim within 300 days of a discriminatory act will be forever barred from bringing an action. The statute of limitations under Section 1981 or 1983, however, is based upon the statute of limitations for personal torts in the state in which the wrong was committed. The limitation period for personal torts in most states is two or three years. An employee is not required to file a claim with the EEOC prior to bringing a lawsuit under Section 1981. Therefore, a claimant who fails to file a timely Title VII charge with the EEOC may still be able to file a timely lawsuit under Section 1981.

Other jurisdictional requirements of Title VII, which may preempt a claim under that Act, do not affect Section 1981 actions. There is no minimum number of employees requirement under Section 1981 and specific Title VII exceptions, such as the bona fide private club exemption, are not available to Section 1981 defendants.

Employees who should give particularly strong consideration to these statutes are those individuals with claims alleging particularly heinous acts by an employer. Punitive damages are possible if the defendant's conduct is shown to be motivated by particularly evil motives or involve reckless disregard for an individual's employment rights. While the damages must have some correlation to the actual injury sustained, large awards have been recovered under these statutes.

While the United States Supreme Court recently upheld the right of employees to use Section 1981 in employment discrimination cases involving race, it limited its ruling to hiring, firing and certain types of promotions. The exclusive federal remedy for racial harassment allegations is Title VII.

NATIONAL ORIGIN

National origin and race complaints generally receive similar analysis. An employee alleging national origin discrimination can cite cases involving racial discrimination to support his allegation. There are at least two situations, however, which are unique to national origin cases: citizenship and language.

The first situation involves individuals who are denied employment because they are not citizens of the United States. While Title VII applies to both documented and undocumented aliens, it does not prohibit discrimination based solely on a lack of United States citizenship. In **Espinoza v. Farah Manufacturing Co., Inc.**, 414 U.S. 86 (1973), the Supreme Court ruled that Congress did not provide protection based on alienage when it passed Title VII. What Congress did provide was protection for certain groups of aliens from discrimination not faced by another group of aliens. For example, an employer is not allowed to give preference to aliens of European heritage over aliens of Hispanic heritage.

The **Espinoza** case involved a situation in which a woman of Mexican ancestry was refused employment in a Texas manufacturing plant because she was not a United States citizen. The employer provided evidence that 96 percent of the employees filling the positions sought by the plaintiff were of Mexican ancestry. The Court was convinced that the employer discriminated against the plaintiff, not based on her national origin, but solely because of her lack of citizenship.

Employers do not have the right to discriminate against aliens in every circumstance, however. The EEOC, adopting language from the **Espinoza** decision, considers discrimination based on citizenship to violate Title VII if the "purpose and effect" of the policy is to discriminate on the basis of national origin. Generally, as in other cases of disparate treatment, Title VII is violated if a policy is adopted as a pretext for discriminating against a protected group. In the **Espinoza** case, for example, had the workforce actually been 96 percent anglo ancestry in a community with a large Hispanic population, it could reasonably be inferred that a citizenship requirement was used to limit Hispanic employment opportunities.

Although alienage is not a per se violation of Title VII, an employee should be aware that other statutes, as well as the 14th Amendment, have been used to invalidate citizenship requirements. The Civil Rights Act of 1866 provides all persons residing in the United States the same rights as white citizens. The Immigration Reform and Control Act of 1986 (IRCA) prohibits knowing and intentional bias because of national origin or citizenship. The IRCA applies to employers having only four employees instead of the 15 employee requirement under Title VII. In addition to discrimination by private employers, many state governments have enacted laws which require United States citizenship or state residency prior to receiving state employment. State laws limiting alien hiring will be upheld only if the position involves a state governmental function, such as police protection, public education or judicial functions. Laws prohibiting alien employment for any state position have been universally invalidated.

While states are not allowed to universally exclude all non-citizens from employment, the federal government is not so limited. In 1976, President Gerald Ford signed Executive Order 11935, which limited all federal civil service positions to United States citizens or nationals, unless specifically excepted by the Civil Service Commission. The order has subsequently been upheld as constitutional.

An employee who believes he has been discriminated against because of alienage should consult with an attorney to determine if protection is provided from statutes other than, or in addition to, Title VII.

A second employment issue unique to national origin cases involves issues dealing with language. Many employers have instituted policies which require that employee conversations be conducted in English. Depending on the type of work involved and the application of the rule, a speak-English-only rule can create a hostile work environment.

Any rule which requires employees to speak English at all times is presumed by the EEOC to be a violation of Title VII. Because an individual's language is often a national origin characteristic, the Commission will find a total prohibition of its use to be a form of national origin harassment. While it is a presumed violation, however, the employer is allowed to show that the rule is justified by a business necessity. Employers have been most successful in defending a total exclusion when the workplace involves dangerous work. An em-

ployer controlling an oil rig, for example, successfully
argued that the danger from possible accidents at
the worksite was so great that employees needed to
maintain communication at all times, even during
breaks. Other situations in which a total exclusion
of foreign languages would probably be upheld include
laboratory work, mining, construction and other haz-
ardous environments.

Non-hazardous work environments do not require
such absolute standards. Employers are allowed to
require English-speaking for customer contacts or
for contacts with English-speaking supervisors. Employers may not require English-speaking during breaks
or private conversations, however. The rule must serve
a legitimate business purpose of productivity, efficiency
or safety.

Efficiency should not be confused with convenience.
An employer which argues that it needs to understand
all employee conversations, even during breaks, must
prove that its employees do better work because of
a speak-English-only rule. It is not enough for an employer to merely state that workers are talking behind
his back.

For the employer that does have a legitimate reason
for a speak-English-only rule, the employer has an
obligation to clearly notify its employees of the rules
it has in effect. Notification can take a variety of
forms, including employee meetings, posters or written
memoranda. The notification should include the precise
hours and locations of the rule, as well as the specific
forms of discipline which will be invoked for violations.

While speak-English-only rules primarily impact
on classes of employees, a number of individual cases
have involved employees with accents affecting their
English-speaking ability. Discrimination because of
an employee's accent violates Title VII when the accent
does not affect an employee's performance on the
job. It is not a violation of Title VII, however, to terminate an employee when the employee's performance
on a job is unsatisfactory because of an inability to
communicate because of an accent. A teacher who
is unable to communicate with students because of

a pronounced accent, for example, could lawfully be terminated even though he has the technical qualifications for the position. The ability to communicate that knowledge is also a requirement for most teaching positions. Cases involving accents will focus on the need for English-fluency in a position and the ability of an employee to successfully fulfill the communication requirements of the job.

AGE DISCRIMINATION

Reduction-in-Force

The exponential increase in the number of ADEA charges is closely related to the decision by many companies in the United States to reduce expenses by cutting back in personnel. The middle managers, comprising the majority of employees typically laid off, are usually over 40 years of age and are well aware of their legal rights. Proving a case under a reduction-in-force situation, however, can differ from the elements required to prove an individual termination case.

As discussed in the disparate treatment section, an employee must initially establish a prima facie case. During a reduction-in-force, he is not required to show that younger workers were retained or that his duties were assumed by a younger worker. To establish a prima facie case, the employee must: (1) show that he is within the protected age group, that is, age 40 or older; (2) show that he was discharged; (3) show that he was qualified for another position; and (4) provide evidence of the employer's intent to discriminate.

One example of a prima facie case is when a company exclusively eliminates positions filled by older employees. In one case, the employer eliminated a number of positions but retained the positions in which younger employees predominated. The court concluded that the terminated employee had established a prima facie case even though he had not personally been replaced by a younger employee.

Although in the prior situation it was relatively easy for an employee to show a prima facie case, it can be more difficult in individual circumstances. In most non-reduction-in-force cases, a competent employee has a built-in prima facie case through evidence of satisfactory job performance as recorded in annual evaluations. In a reduction-in-force case, however, an employee is required to show not only that he was a competent employee in the past but that he could also adapt to the requirements of a new management philosophy. Employees with good evaluations, but with questions as to their ability to change, may find themselves without a claim.

Once an employee provides evidence of a prima facie case, the employer must articulate a legitimate defense. The usual articulation by the employer in these cases is that economic reasons necessitated the closing of an office, the elimination of personnel, or the reduction in costs or losses.

After the employer offers an explanation for its actions, the employee must prove that the employer's explanation is not the real reason for the termination. The employee must provide some evidence, either direct, circumstantial or statistical, that age was a determining factor.

Courts will rarely challenge a business determination to reduce the size of a workforce. An employee with evidence that the employer considered replacing him **prior** to the reduction, however, can show that the reduction-in-force was merely an attempt by the employer to legitimize a discriminatory act. Evidence of discriminatory intent prior to the reduction, although not usually existing, is very powerful if available.

The terminated employee should initially compare himself to employees within the department in which he worked. While a terminated employee must show that he was qualified for a position which remained after the reduction, the employer is under no duty to transfer an employee into a position held by a younger employee. The ADEA does not require seniority bumping rights. The more usual scenario, however, is that younger employees will be allowed to transfer to other departments or locations while older employees are discharged. One of the major stereotypes the ADEA was promoted to remedy is the notion that older employees are unable to adapt to changing circumstances. The first focus, therefore, should be on whether the employee was qualified for a position in which there was a transfer or change of duties.

If no position is found, the employee will be required to show either direct evidence that age played a role in the termination decisions (such as memos or statements by the employer) or prove statistically that the decisions were age-biased (see disparate impact).

Use of Salary Information

Especially in reduction-in-force situations, employers are primarily interested in reducing expenses. Therefore, when employers decide which employees to retain, the high salaried employees often receive the highest level of scrutiny.

The problem, however, is that in many situations the use of salary in termination decisions violates the ADEA. That is primarily because of the usual relationship between an employee's salary and his length of service with a company.

It is still the employee's burden to prove his case. The fact that an employee can establish that he was dismissed because of his salary is not enough to prove age discrimination. He must also show that his age or length of service with the company is reflected by his salary. In most cases, this is easily shown through payroll records which detail annual or periodic raises throughout an employment history.

The more frequent problem is proving that salary was the motivating factor behind an employer's decision to terminate an employee. One strategy is the process of elimination. When the terminated employee's evaluations are equal to or better than his younger retained counterparts, salary may be the only remaining discrepancy. Most jurors bring with them an understanding that employers seek to keep expenses as low as possible, adding credence to the employee's argument. Needless to say, the larger the disparity in salaries, the greater the inference the employer used such information in its decision. There is one major exception to the prohibition against the use of salary in termination decisions. When the survival of the company is at stake, the burden is on the employer to show that no other cost-cutting measures were available prior to the termination of high-salaried employees.

Bias on the basis of salary and/or seniority is not, on its face, bias as a result of age. In the recent past, courts have held that salary could be used in discharge cases involving a one-on-one employee comparison. Only when salary was used in determinations involving large numbers of employees was it found unlawful. The recent trend, however, is to disallow the use of salary in any circumstances in which the employee can show that his high salary was primarily a result of the length of service with the company.

SEXUAL HARASSMENT

Title VII prohibits unwelcome sexual advances or conduct in the workplace. One of the most widespread but least alleged types of employment discrimination, sexual harassment claims have gradually increased in recent years and may be the major employment issue of the 1990's.

Although the most widely-recognized form of sexual harassment is that by a male supervisor against a female subordinate, it is possible for either a man or a woman to be a victim, and a woman as well as a man to be the harasser. The harasser could be the victim's supervisor, an agent of the employer, another supervisor, a co-worker, or a non-employee, such as a customer or repair person. The victim need not necessarily be a member of the opposite sex of the harasser. A court's primary focus is whether the harasser treats a member or members of one sex differently from those of the opposite sex. Therefore, sexual harassment can result if the harasser and victim are of the same sex, and the harasser does not treat members of the opposite sex in a similar fashion. Individuals other than the person against whom the sexual conduct is directed also can be victims. If the sexual harassment of one employee creates an intimidating, hostile, or offensive environment for a co-worker who is not the object of sexual advances, then the co-worker is a victim. In a recent decision, **Broderick v. Ruder**, 685 F. Supp. 1269 (D.D.C. 1988), an attorney for the federal government won her sexual harassment claim even though she was not the primary target of sexual advances. What she did not receive was career advancement enjoyed by co-workers who were involved in relationships with agency supervisors. The court concluded that the consensual affairs of her co-workers created a sexually hostile working environment that "affected the motivation and work performance of those who found such conduct repugnant and offensive." The court held the government agency liable because it had knowledge of the conduct.

An employer is only liable for harassment about which it is aware. There are two primary ways in which an employer will gain such knowledge. In most cases, the victim complains to a management official, at which point the employer has direct knowledge of the violation. According to some company policies, victims of harassment are required to notify their immediate supervisors of harassing situations. A victim is not required to complain to their supervisor, however, if the supervisor is the harasser. The fact that a victim fails to notify anyone in the company, however, will not automatically defeat a claim. If the harassment is prolonged or pervasive, or if it is widely known throughout the workplace, then the employer will be considered to have constructive knowledge of the harassment and will be liable for damages unless it promptly and decisively corrects the activity.

An economic injury, such as a loss of a promotion or job, is not necessary to a finding of sexual harassment. All that is required is for the harasser to unreasonably interfere with the victim's work performance or create

an intimidating, hostile, harmful or offensive work
environment. Types of conduct which can create a
hostile work environment include oppressive workloads,
unwarranted criticism, public humiliation and undesirable
job transfers.

Harassment involves **unwelcome** sexual advances,
requests for sexual favors, or verbal or physical conduct
of a sexual nature. An advance will be considered
unwelcome if one of three criteria is met: (1) the
harasser makes submission to the conduct an explicit
or implicit term or condition of the victim's employment;
(2) submission to or rejection of the conduct by the
victim is the basis for an employment decision affecting
the victim; or (3) the conduct unreasonably interferes
with the victim's work performance or creates an
intimidating, hostile or offensive work environment.
The issue is whether the sexual advances are unwelcome,
not whether the participation of a victim is voluntary.
An employee who submits to unwelcome sexual advances
does not necessarily relinquish his or her Title VII
protection.

Employees should be aware that sexual harassment
complaints can lead to state law actions in addition
to Title VII. Lawsuits alleging assault and battery
or the intentional infliction of emotional distress often
provide plaintiffs with an opportunity to recover compensatory and punitive damages, damages that are
not available under Title VII. Most large damage awards
in this area will include some type of state civil
action.

It is in the employer's best interest to make efforts
to prevent sexual harassment before it occurs. Suggested
preventive steps include raising the subject of sexual
harassment, expressing strong disapproval, developing
appropriate sanctions, educating employees on how
to assert their right to be free from sexual harassment
and making everyone more sensitive to the issue. Once
an employer learns of a charge of harassment, prompt
investigation and action to remedy the situation will
limit its liability.

PREGNANCY

On October 31, 1978, President Jimmy Carter signed into law the Pregnancy Discrimination Act (PDA) as an amendment to Title VII. Even before Section 701(k) was added to Title VII, an employer was prohibited from basing hiring decisions on pregnancy, childbirth or related medical conditions. What the PDA added was a requirement that employers include pregnancy coverage to existing sick leave and medical insurance policies.

In general terms, the PDA requires that persons affected by pregnancy, childbirth and related medical conditions be treated the same as employees suffering from other types of disabilities. An employer that extends short- or long-term disability coverage for other disorders must include such coverage for pregnancy-related disabilities. An employer that provides medical coverage for illness must also insure the medical expenses of pregnant employees. The PDA does not require an employer to provide these types of plans, it just requires employers to include pregnancy-related conditions if it chooses to do so in other areas.

Although Title VII has always protected pregnant women as to hirings, firings, promotions and seniority, the PDA affirmed the prohibition against employer stereotypes that women become pregnant and leave the labor market. The PDA, while not guaranteeing financial relief, protects the right of a woman to leave the labor force while disabled from pregnancy-related conditions.

Pregnant women have the right to work for as long as their health permits. An employer cannot force an employee to accept sick or disability leave just because she becomes pregnant. It is no defense to allege that customer preference requires that pregnant employees be placed on leave. In fact, a pregnant woman has the right to have her job assignments modified to the extent an employer modifies the assignments of other employees suffering from other disabilities. A pregnant woman whose job requires some heavy lifting can have those duties modified if employees with temporary back problems, for example, have had their lifting requirements modified in the past. While women have the right to work before a baby is born, they also have the right to return to work after a baby is born. A woman who leaves a job due to pregnancy has the right to have her job held open on the same basis as jobs held open for employees who leave because of illness. Although unsettled law, the EEOC prohibits employers from terminating pregnant employees even if its policy is to terminate every other employee that takes a break in service. EEOC Guidelines require employers to provide "reasonable" amounts of leave to pregnant employees, usually considered four to eight weeks, unless the employer has a business necessity to require uninterrupted service. The most likely business necessity occurs when employment is for a short period of time and leave of four to eight weeks would create a severe hardship to a company. For continuing operations, however, reasonable leave is required.

While an employer is required to extend reasonable maternity leave, leave is required only for the period of time in which a woman is physically disabled. The PDA does not require an employer to grant leave to an employee for non-required absences. An employer is not allowed to require a company physician to certify the disability, however, unless examinations by a company doctor are also required as a condition for continued employment by non-pregnant employees returning from disabilities. In most cases, a report from a woman's personal physician must be accepted.

A reasonable period of leave does not extend to a reasonable period of paid leave, however. Paid leaves are required only to the extent that employees suffering from other disabilities receive paid leave. An employer that cuts off benefits at a maximum dollar level for non-pregnancy related disabilities may also cut off pregnancy benefits at an equivalent level.

A few collateral issues have evolved due to the moral and ethical considerations inherent in subjects involving reproduction. While an employer may desire to discourage pregnancy among single employees, it is only allowed to discriminate against single parents if a primary function of the organization is to provide role models for young people. Most employers, therefore, are not allowed to limit pregnancy insurance to married employees. Organizations such as the Girl Scouts or Girl's Clubs, however, may terminate unmarried employees who become pregnant. The role model function must be a primary function, however. School districts, for example, whose primary function is education, have not been allowed to fire pregnant teachers due to their unmarried status.

The PDA specifically excludes abortions from required insurance coverage unless the life of the mother would be endangered by carrying the baby to full term. Complications arising from abortions, however, must be insured to the extent that other disabilities are covered by medical insurance. Nothing in the Act prevents companies from providing coverage for abortions, however, should they so desire.

Employers may protect fetuses from unhealthy work environments. Lead, for example, is a proven cause of deformities and retardation in infants born to mothers with high levels in their blood. Under these circumstances, an employer may limit the positions to employees who are unable to bear children. The fact that a woman states that she does not intend to become pregnant, or offers to sign an agreement releasing the employer from liability should she do so, will not affect the prohibition. Not all pregnancies are planned, and under the law a woman cannot release the rights of her unborn child. An employer is required to modify the positions if possible, however, prior to adopting a total prohibition.

RELIGIOUS ACCOMMODATION

Title VII prohibits discrimination against a person on the basis of his religious beliefs. The definition of religion includes all aspects of sincerely held religious observances, practices and beliefs. Non-traditional as well as traditional religious practices are protected. EEOC regulations define religious practices to include moral and ethical beliefs of an individual if they are sincerely held with the strength of traditional religious views. This standard was developed by the Supreme Court in **United States v. Seeger,** 380 U.S. 163 (1965), and **Welsh v. United States,** 398 U.S. 333 (1970). The fact that no religious group espouses such beliefs, or the fact that the religious group to which an individual professes to belong may not accept such beliefs, is not determinative of whether the belief is sincerely held. The fact that an individual actually lives his life under a particular set of standards is enough to qualify such beliefs as a religion under the Act.

Once an employee has such a belief and notifies his employer or labor union of the need for a religious accommodation, the employer or union is under a duty to reasonably accommodate the individual's religious practices. The employer or union may refuse to accommodate the employee if each available alternative would cause an undue hardship on the business. The employer or union may not avoid accommodating an employee, however, by merely assuming that many other people with similar religious practices may also need a similar accommodation.

Allegations of religious discrimination most often arise when an individual's work schedule conflicts with his observance of a Sabbath. Many conflicts have occurred when an employee is scheduled to work on Saturdays, and the employee observes Saturday as a religious day of rest. One possible accommodation would be to allow the employee to arrange to have another employee of substantially similar qualifications to substitute for him. The employee could then arrange to work one of the days the substitute is scheduled.

The employer is not required to make the arrangements for an exchange. That is the employee's obligation. The employer must, however, make a minimal effort to facilitate such a substitution. The employer could, for example, help the employee by publicizing company policies regarding reasonable accommodation and voluntary substitution or swapping. The employer could promote or support such substitutions so that its employees regard them favorably. A bulletin board or other means for arranging voluntary substitutions often is provided by an employer to meet this statutory burden.

Another means of providing reasonable accommodation is the creation of flexible scheduling. Flexible scheduling might include flexible arrival and departure times; floating or optional holidays; flexible work breaks; loss of lunch time in exchange for early departure; staggered work hours; permitting an employee to make up time lost because of religious observance; or permitting an employee to take time off without pay.

Religious accommodation does not just involve scheduling conflicts. A frequent request for accommodation occurs when an employee's religious beliefs do not permit him to join, or pay dues to, a labor union, as required by some collective bargaining agreements. The union can accommodate such an employee by not requiring him to join or by allowing him to donate a sum equivalent to the dues to a charitable organization.

While an employer is required to accommodate an employee's religious beliefs, its burden is only slight. An employer may refuse to accommodate an employee if to do so would result in more than "de minimis" or minimal cost. For example, a cost of paying premium overtime wages was considered by the Supreme Court to cause undue hardship in **Trans World Airlines v. Hardison**, 432 U.S. 63 (1977). Administrative costs incurred in rearranging schedules and recording substitutions for payroll purposes would not cause undue hardship, however.

Undue hardships also result when an employer must vary a bona fide seniority system in order to accommodate an employee. An employer may not deny another employee a job or shift preference guaranteed by the seniority system. Voluntary substitutions or swaps, however, even if violating a bona fide seniority system, do not cause an undue hardship. A provision may be included in collective bargaining agreements to allow voluntary substitutions or swaps.

An employer must make reasonable accommodations at the pre-employment or selection stage of the hiring process. If a test is scheduled at a time when an employee or prospective employee cannot attend for religious reasons, the employer is required to re-issue the test unless to do so would cause undue hardship. If an applicant for a position would require accommodation should he be hired, an employer may not allow this need to affect its hiring decision.

Employers should be cautious in questioning applicants about their availability to work specific shifts and dates. Such inquiries may limit the employment opportunities of those with certain religious practices and will provide damaging evidence once a charge is filed. To avoid violating Title VII, an employer must be able to show that the inquiries did not have an exclusionary effect on employees or prospective employees needing an accommodation. Alternatively, the employer must be able to show that the inquiries were justified by business necessity. According to the regulations published by the EEOC, the Commission will infer religious discrimination against a rejected applicant if an employer asks about the applicant's availability prior to making an offer of employment without there being a business necessity justification. Discrimination will also be inferred if the employer rejects a qualified applicant after determining the applicant's need for an accommodation.

Once a court infers that discrimination influenced an employer's actions, the burden shifts to the employer to demonstrate that factors other than the need for an accommodation were the reasons behind rejecting a qualified applicant, i.e., the employer could not reasonably accommodate the applicant without undue hardship.

Under Title VII, religious accommodation by an employer extends to the religious-oriented dress and grooming practices of its employees. Examples of religious dress practices include the wearing or non-wearing of particular articles of clothing such as hats, turbans, shirts, gowns, dresses or pants. Additionally, religious grooming practices may include prescribed hair styles, facial hair or make-up. Conforming to these religious practices may violate an employer's dress code. As with other aspects of religious practice, an employer may refuse to accommodate the employee or prospective employee only if the employer can demonstrate that to do so would cause it undue hardship. An employer that required snug fitting respirators during work, for example, was not required to retain an employee who wore a beard for religious purposes.

AFFIRMATIVE ACTION

When Congress enacted Title VII, it sought to improve the economic and social conditions of minorities and women by providing equality of opportunity in the workplace. Conditions in the workplace often reflected a pattern of restriction, exclusion, discrimination, segregation and inferior treatment of minorities and women. To address these conditions, Congress, through Title VII, established a national policy against employment discrimination based on race, color, religion, sex and national origin. In addition, Congress sought to have employers, labor organizations and other persons subject to Title VII voluntarily modify their employment practices to correct the effects of past discrimination and prevent present and future discrimination. To assist employers in their efforts, the EEOC published guidelines describing the circumstances in which those subject to Title VII may take or agree upon voluntary action to improve employment opportunities for minorities and women.

Certain circumstances must be present before voluntary affirmative action is appropriate. An employer subject to Title VII may take affirmative action steps to modify practices, procedures or policies when they have an adverse impact on minorities and women. Actions also may be instituted to correct the effects of past discriminatory practices. Past effects can be identified by comparing the employer's workforce, or a part of it, with an appropriate segment of the labor force. The percentage of minorities and women in the workforce should resemble the pool of available minorities and women available for employment. A significant discrepancy could justify affirmative action in such areas as training plans and programs in recruiting, the elimination of unvalidated selection criteria and/or modification of promotion and layoff procedures. The modification can be carried out either through collective bargaining, if a labor organization represents employees, or unilaterally, where there is no such labor agreement.

An affirmative action plan must contain three elements. These are a reasonable self analysis, a reasonable basis for concluding action is appropriate and reasonable action.

The employer should initially conduct a self analysis to determine whether its practices do, or tend to, exclude, disadvantage or restrict the employment opportunities of minority employees. If its workforce is unbalanced, the employer should attempt to determine whether the result was caused by present or historical discrimination. The problem may have resulted from discrimination by other persons or institutions, or may be the effects of present employment practices.

An employer has a reasonable basis for concluding an affirmative action plan is appropriate if the self analysis reveals employment practices which have or tend to have an adverse effect on employment opportunities for members of previously excluded groups or groups whose opportunities have been artificially limited. There is a reasonable basis for a plan if employment practices leave uncorrected the effects of prior discrimination, or if they result in disparate treatment. There can be a reasonable basis even without an admission or a formal finding that the employer has violated Title VII, and despite any arguable defenses to a Title VII action.

When an employer determines that an affirmative action plan is required or desirable, its actions must be reasonable in relation to the problems revealed during the self analysis. Reasonable action may include goals and timetables which recognize the race, sex or national origin of applicants or employees. The employer may adopt practices to eliminate the actual or potential adverse impact, disparate treatment, or effect of past discrimination by providing opportunities for members of groups which have been excluded in the past. These steps may be taken regardless of whether the persons benefitting from the plan were themselves the victims of prior discriminatory policies or procedures.

An affirmative action plan tailored to the problems identified in the employer's self analysis should avoid unnecessary restrictions on the opportunities of nonminority employees. The employer can maintain the race, sex and national origin conscious provision only so long as necessary to achieve the objectives of the plan. Goals and timetables must be reasonably related to the effects of past discrimination, the need for prompt elimination of adverse impact or disparate treatment, the availability of basically qualified applicants or those who can become qualified, and the number of employment opportunities expected to be available.

If an employee or applicant goes to court to challenge an employment decision made pursuant to an affirmative action plan, he has the burden of establishing the invalidity of the plan. In examining the decision and whether it was based on a valid plan, the initial consideration is whether an imbalance exists to justify taking sex or race into account. The imbalance must exist in **traditionally** segregated job categories in order to assure that sex and race will be taken into account in a manner consistent with Title VII's goal of eliminating the effects of discrimination. A comparison of the percentage of minorities or women in the employer's workforce with the percentage in the area labor market or general population is necessary in analyzing jobs requiring no special expertise. If special training is necessary, then the comparison is made to those in the labor force who possess the relevant qualifications.

A second consideration is whether the affirmative action plan unnecessarily trammels the rights of nonminorities or creates an absolute bar to their advancement. A plan which merely authorizes that consideration be given to affirmative action concerns when evaluating

qualified applicants rather than setting quotas is prefer-
able. In this way, no one is automatically excluded
from consideration, and everyone is able to have his
qualifications weighed against those of other applicants.
If a plan does set aside a specific number of positions
for minorities and women, it should expressly provide
that such a program is only temporary. That will mini-
mize the program's effect on other employees and
ensure that it is used not to achieve and maintain
racial and sexual balance but rather as a benchmark
against which an employer may measure its progress
in remedying past discrimination.

To date, affirmative action plans have only been
upheld in hiring or promotion settings. An affirmative
action plan affecting labor force reductions will probably
be held to infringe upon the employment rights of
terminated employees.

According to the Supreme Court, Section 706(g)
of Title VII does not allow a court to order a remedy
for an individual who was not a victim of discrimination.
However, a court may order affirmative race-conscious
relief as a remedy for past bias, even if the relief
benefits those not discriminated against.

HEIGHT AND WEIGHT REQUIREMENTS

Height and weight requirements, although appearing
to be non-discriminatory, often violate Title VII. According to national statistics, women on the average are
not as tall as, nor weigh as much as, men. Therefore,
if an employer requires a minimum weight or height,
women are likely to be disproportionately excluded.
In **Dothard v. Rawlinson,** 433 U.S. 321 (1977), the United
States Supreme Court determined that an employer's
minimum height requirement of 67 inches unlawfully
excluded more women than men from consideration.
Women, on average, had a height of 63 inches, while
the average height of men was 68.2 inches. The Supreme
Court concluded that Title VII was intended to eliminate
this sort of artificial and unnecessary barrier to
employment.

Height and weight requirements may be analyzed under the disparate treatment or disparate impact theory. Disparate treatment results when an employer maintains a height and weight requirement but enforces it only against a particular group or class. An example would be if an employer strictly applies height and weight requirements to black applicants but makes frequent exceptions for white applicants. The non-uniform application of its requirements would result in unlawful discrimination. Another example of disparate treatment is having one minimum height requirement for women or Hispanics, such as 5'5", and a higher minimum height requirement for other applicants, such as 5'8". In this example, a 5'7" Caucasian male would be excluded because of his sex or national origin. A similarly situated woman or Hispanic would not be excluded.

Disparate impact results from a minimum height or weight requirement that is neutral on its face and is applied equally to all protected groups or classes. The effect of this type of requirement would be to disproportionately exclude significant numbers of employees within a protected group. As discussed above, minimum height or weight requirements may exclude women, Hispanics or Asians from consideration who, based on national statistics, are on the average shorter than men or individuals of other national origins or races.

In challenging a minimum height requirement, an applicant must initially establish a prima facie case. This must be accomplished through the use of national statistics showing a disproportionate exclusion of members of a protected group. The employer must then state a legitimate reason for the height requirement based on business necessity.

Minimum weight requirements primarily impact on women. The belief that heavier people are stronger often leads employers to impose minimum weight requirements for positions requiring heavy lifting. Again, for an employer to defend such a requirement, it must be able to show business necessity. If heavy lifting is required for a position, an employer will be required to conduct less restrictive strength tests prior to imposing minimum weight requirements.

Airlines are the employers which most frequently impose maximum weight limits. Flight attendants are often limited to a maximum weight which is in proportion to their height and body frame. Courts have generally held that, because a person is able to control his or her body weight, weight is not an immutable characteristic protected by Title VII. Different maximum weights for men and women of the same height are permissible because of physiological differences between men and women. Even in this situation, however, limits may not be set so that a significantly greater proportion of women are excluded from the applicant pool.

GROOMING AND APPEARANCE

There are a variety of employment issues within the subject of grooming and appearance. Many complaints have resulted from the natural differences in the dress and appearance of the sexes. While Title VII requires that employees be treated equally, it cannot require that employees dress identically. Situations in which the differences violate the Act are discussed below.

Hair

Many claims have been filed by men alleging sex discrimination under Title VII against employers which allow women, but not men, to wear long hair. The complaints have been met with universal disapproval by the courts. Some courts treat hair length as a mutable characteristic, that is, a characteristic which an individual can readily change. These courts have held that different restrictions for men and women, therefore, do not come within the purview of Title VII. Other courts based their findings on the fact that employers may set grooming codes for both sexes. Despite the fact that the codes may not be identical, an employer that enforces a certain style of dress for both sexes, conservative for example, will be able to dictate a reasonable length of hair for its employees. Although there are no court opinions on point, a recent complaint was settled in which black women were disciplined for wearing their hair in tight braids or "cornrows." The women filed a complaint alleging that their hairstyle was a characteristic of their national origin. The case was successfully settled when the women convinced the company that the hairstyle, when neatly braided, did not violate company policies requiring a conservative appearance.

Facial Hair

Men have been unsuccessful in challenging employer no-beard policies on the basis of sex discrimination. Since wearing a beard is based on personal preference, courts have found that facial hair is a mutable characteristic which will not lead to a valid disparate impact claim.

Black males, however, have been successful in challenging no-beard policies because of a condition known as pseudo-folliculitis barbae (PFB), which requires individuals to refrain from shaving. According to an EEOC study, 50 percent of black males have PFB, 25 percent of whom suffer to the degree that they are unable to shave. PFB afflicts only 1 percent of white males.

For those who suffer from PFB, the failure to shave is not personal preference, but medical necessity. Early plaintiffs who attempted to argue this theory were usually unsuccessful, however, as a result of the failure to undertake the expensive studies required to prove disparate impact. The EEOC study cited in Commission Decision 83-17, however, will probably validate future claims using this argument.

Companies can enforce no-beard rules on employees who are not afflicted by PFB. For those inflicted, however, the employer will be required to show business necessity prior to enforcing its policy. One retail food chain has been successful in arguing that it is necessary for its employees to be clean shaven for reasons of hygiene and to retain customers. While customer preference is not a valid business justification for hiring a white applicant over a black applicant, customer preference for clean shaven employees will be a minimum requirement to validate a no-beard policy. It is still to be determined whether customer preference alone will persuade other courts that Title VII has not been violated. As has always been the rule, however, companies may require beards to be neat and trimmed.

Dress Codes

Dress codes do not violate Title VII as long as they are enforced equally against both sexes. While dress codes must be equally applied, the specific requirements for each sex may differ. Therefore, an employer that requires its male employees to wear coats and ties is not required to demand identical attire for its female employees. It would be required to set a similar conservative standard for both sexes, however.

An employer is allowed to exercise its legitimate concern for the business image created by its employees' appearances. A national case involving personal appearance was **Craft v. Metromedia, Inc.,** 575 F. Supp. 868 (1983). Ms. Craft, a television news anchorwoman, accused her employer of sex discrimination when it demoted her to a reporting role because of her failure to comply with a rigorous dress code. She also complained that she received constant criticism regarding her appearance, while her male counterparts were not treated by the same standards.

According to the district court, Title VII was never intended to interfere with the institution and enforcement of personal appearance regulations. The court decided that the television station did not discriminate against Ms. Craft on the basis of her sex, because both men and women were required to maintain professional, businesslike appearances consistent with community standards. The court held that since television is a visual medium, it requires a strict appearance code to preserve the economic well-being of the station.

Even though employers may institute dress codes, they may not do so based on stereotypes. Discrimination was found in a case involving a bank which required women to wear uniforms, but allowed men to wear suitable business attire. The employer failed to present evidence to show that the women had worn improper business attire on the days when their uniforms were being cleaned. The court concluded that the bank's justification for the uniform requirement, namely that women were less capable of selecting appropriate business attire, was based on stereotypes prohibited by Title VII.

While dress codes are not required to be in writing, unwritten codes invite litigation. Employers without official codes, however, may still enforce minimum standards of attire. In one case, a female employee wore a halter top to a job in which there had been no previous dress requirements. The employer informed her that halter tops were nonetheless inappropriate even for the warehouse. When the employee refused to change her clothes, she was terminated. In rejecting her Title VII claim, the court held that a business has a right to be concerned with its image and can set minimum standards without violating the Act. It should be noted, however, that in situations without a dress code, the employees should first be warned prior to disciplinary action.

While sexually suggestive attire may violate employer standards, employer standards which require the wearing of sexually suggestive attire also may violate Title VII. One California court found a violation of Title VII when a bar discharged a cocktail waitress for failing to wear suggestive dresses. Just as clearly, employers may not require secretaries and office staff to wear sexually suggestive attire without violating Title VII. A restaurant that has a liberal uniform will more likely have its requirement upheld. Employers that require suggestive attire for only female employees, however, leave themselves open to charges of sexual discrimination.

Conservative attire has not received the same judicial response. Employers may require men to wear

neckties and prohibit women from wearing slacks in
executive offices if a dress code is applied equally
to both sexes. If reasonable, an employer may institute
dress codes it deems appropriate.

EQUAL PAY ACT

The EPA is divided into two parts. The first section
prohibits discrimination within any establishment,
"on the basis of sex by paying wages to employees
of the opposite sex in such an establishment for equal
work on jobs the performance of which requires equal
skill, effort, and responsibility, and which are performed
under similar working conditions." The second section
authorizes salary differentiations where the payment
is made pursuant to (i) a seniority system; (ii) a merit
system; (iii) a system based on quality or quantity
of production; or (iv) a differential based on any other
factor other than sex.

The burden of proof, therefore, is a two-step process,
unlike the three-step process required to prove Title
VII disparate treatment cases. The initial burden is
on the employee to show wage disparity and job equality.
Wage disparity is usually the easiest to prove. Wages
include salaries, bonuses and benefits, such as the
use of an automobile or pension contributions. Job
equality, which includes mental as well as physical
labors, is addressed in greater detail later in this section.

Once a plaintiff proves wage disparity and job
equality, the burden shifts to the employer to rebut
the job equality evidence or assert one of the four
EPA defenses. Unlike disparate treatment analysis
under Title VII, in which the employee always retains
the ultimate burden of proof, the EPA requires that
the employer prove that its non-discriminatory defense
is legitimate.

The EPA's first three defenses are already included
in Title VII. Seniority systems, merit systems or systems
in which the quality or quantity of work can be
measured typically can be readily judged. Seniority
and merit systems require more scrutiny, however,

to determine whether they have been non-discrimi-
natorily managed. A system which rewards membership
in a community organization which discriminates against
women, for example, will not produce a bona fide
merit system defense.

As could be expected, the majority of litigation
involves the fourth statutory defense—a differential
based on any factor other than sex. The most typical
defenses include experience, education, responsibilities
or seniority. There is no marketplace defense, however.
An employer may not claim that it hired a woman
at a lower wage because women accept lower wages
than men. This is the type of discrimination that the
EPA was enacted to prohibit.

Equal Skill, Effort and Responsibility

Under the EPA, the jobs in comparison need not
be identical, only "substantially equal" in skill, effort
and responsibility. Examples of positions which have
been held to be substantially equal include barbers
and beauticians, pursers and stewardesses, managers
of different departments within one retail establishment,
and a female intramural sports director with a small
college basketball coach.

Obviously the easiest comparison is made when
two positions involve identical work. Even in this situation, however, the responsibilities of one of the parties
may prevent a successful EPA claim. Although a shop
supervisor and his assistant may actually perform
the same types of physical labor, a supervisor with
ultimate authority over the final product may be paid
more for the heightened accountability.

The fact that an employee actually performs extra
duties will not necessarily defeat an EPA action, however. If additional duties performed by males are
economically less valuable than the normal duties
performed by both sexes, the added duties ordinarily
cannot be used to legitimize a higher wage. If order
packers are paid five dollars per hour, for example,
and order movers are paid four dollars per hour, the
fact that males may also help with moving would not

justify higher salaries than those paid full-time female packers who do not help with moving.

Closely related to the extra duty defense is an employer's claim of increased job flexibility. Employers are allowed to pay higher wages to employees if their specialized talents allow an employer increased flexibility in work assignments. Although this increased flexibility need not actually be used, there must be a "reasonable possibility" that the employee will be called upon to use the additional skill responsible for a higher wage.

Just as positions are not required to be identical, a male with whom a female is compared need not be employed at an identical time. Jobs may be compared in succession as well as simultaneously. A female who replaces a male in a position may compare her salary to that which the male would have made had he remained employed, including any prospective raises.

Equal pay for equal work does not convert to equal pay for comparable work. Comparable worth is a relatively recent legal theory in which women have alleged violations of the EPA and Title VII based on historically low wages in predominately female professions. In **Lemons v. City and County of Denver**, 620 F. 2d 228 (10th Cir. 1980), nurses filed a complaint alleging that they were paid less than other city employees, such as sanitation workers, even though their positions were comparable in worth. Neither the EPA nor Title VII forces employers to assess the worth of employees or pay market rates.

If a complainant discovers that the jobs being compared are not substantially equal in skill, effort and responsibility, but still believes that the salary was based on intentional discrimination, she should file a complaint under Title VII. An employer which states that "no woman will make as much as a man" is a classic example of a situation in which a substantially similar comparison will not be required under Title VII. Under the EPA, however, this example would not state a cause of action.

Same Establishment

The EPA specifies that comparisons for equality be made between jobs within the same establishment. The same establishment rule protects employers which maintain plants in different areas of the country and thereby maintain separate wage scales. Different departments within a store or separate agencies within a state, city or county employer are considered one unit for EPA purposes, however. Physically separate work places can be considered one establishment if managers and decisionmakers exert control over both facilities. Nationwide lawsuits, however, must be brought under Title VII, which does not have the same establishment limitation.

RETALIATION

Employees who file charges of discrimination are provided the broadest scope of protection within the Acts. Title VII, the ADEA and EPA all prohibit employers from taking adverse employment actions against employees who file charges of discrimination or participate in investigations of discrimination.

The ability of an agency to investigate charges of discrimination is strongly influenced by the amount of cooperation provided by company officials and employees. When one employee is disciplined for participating in an investigation, other employees are less likely to cooperate. The EEOC, therefore, is more likely to file an early lawsuit or render an early determination on this type of claim than on any other.

According to the Acts, employers may not discriminate against individuals who "oppose" practices made unlawful by the Acts or "participate" in EEOC or company investigations. The most common form of opposition is the filing of a complaint or charge with a federal or state agency. The opposition clause does not just protect employees who file federal complaints. Employees who threaten to file complaints are similarly protected. The opposition need not take a formal appearance.

Most types of opposition are protected. An employee protesting alleged discriminatory practices by picketing outside company offices, for example, was held to be protected by the opposition clause of Title VII. Not all employee conduct is protected, however. An employee who dynamites his supervisor's home, for example, will not be covered whether his intent is to oppose discrimination or not. As a rule, opposition to discriminatory practices must be lawful and non-violent.

An employee is not required to prove that an original charge of discrimination was true prior to being afforded protection from retaliation. The only prerequisite regarding the original charge is that it be made in good faith. Although some courts have even shielded employees who filed false or malicious claims, employees who file unfounded claims merely to harass an employer will likely receive little assistance from either the courts or the EEOC. Most courts require that an employee have a good faith belief that he was the victim of discrimination.

As in disparate treatment cases, an employee must initially show a prima facie case of retaliatory treatment. To establish a prima facie case of retaliation, the employee must show: (1) he engaged in protected activity which is known by the employer; (2) an adverse employment action occurred; and (3) there is a causal connection between the two. The causal connection will most likely be shown by a short time period between a protected act, such as the filing of a charge, and an adverse employment action, such as a termination or demotion. An employee who has consistently good evaluations, but receives an unsatisfactory mark after filing a complaint, will generally meet the prima facie burden. Adverse actions taking place two years or more after the filing of a complaint, however, will probably not meet the plaintiff's prima facie burden without additional proof that discrimination actually occurred.

It is crucial to a retaliation complaint that the employee show the employer knew of his opposition to discriminatory practices. An employee that complains of an adverse employment action suffered by a black co-worker, for example, but never complains that it was racially related, has opposed unfair practices, not discriminatory practices. Likewise, an employee that complains about discriminatory practices to co-workers, but not to the supervisor who made the adverse employment decision, will have to prove that the employer knew of his opposition. This is not to say that the opposition need be intentional. An employee who tells a black individual to apply with his employer, and is then terminated for recommending undesirables, is still protected by the opposition clause whether the act was intended to oppose discrimination or not. What is important is whether the **employer** viewed it as opposition at the time of its adverse action.

Once an employee makes out a prima facie case, the analysis is identical to that in other disparate treatment cases. The employer must articulate a non-discriminatory reason for an adverse employment action, after which the employee must show that the articulated reason is a pretext for discrimination.

Although retaliation provisions provide broad protection, they do not provide security to employees already facing discipline for unsatisfactory job performance. On occasion, an employee facing legitimate employer discipline will file a charge with the EEOC to give the impression that an employer's normal disciplinary action is retaliatory. The retaliation provisions were not designed to prevent employers from making legitimate non-discriminatory employment decisions.

There are also certain jobs within a company in which the employee's conduct in opposing discriminatory practices must take a non-inflammatory form. One of the job requirements of corporate executives and EEO officers, for example, is to defuse hostile employment situations. When the manner of opposing discrimination is in direct conflict with an employee's job duties, the employee must use good judgment in expressing his opposition. A corporate executive who uses a public meeting to express his dissatisfaction with company discrimination policies, for example, will not usually be protected by the opposition clause.

Likewise, EEO officers hired to resolve complaints within a company framework may not use their inside positions to collect information for public complaints. Only when all other avenues have failed will these employees be allowed to make public complaints and maintain Title VII and ADEA protection.

In most situations, however, the scope of Section 704(a) protection under Title VII and Section 4(d) of the ADEA is described as "exceptionally broad." An employer may not refuse to hire an employee just because he filed a charge against another employer. An employer that is successful in defending a complaint may not relay that fact to a second employer conducting a reference check. Discriminatory referrals are a significant source of retaliation complaints. Employers which have had discrimination complaints filed against them subject themselves to litigation if they are the source of that information becoming public.

V.
Statute of Limitations

A statute of limitations requires a party to take an action within a fixed period of time or be forever barred from enforcing a claim. There are two specific statute of limitation periods which are important for employment discrimination purposes. The first involves filing a charge with the EEOC; the second with filing a lawsuit in state or federal court.

Under both Title VII and the ADEA, the limitations period for filing a charge begins to run once the employee receives notice of a discriminatory act, not when the harm of the act manifests itself. Therefore, a verbal notification of a future discharge would start the time running, even if the company policy is to provide written notice. The failure of a company to provide written notice does not excuse an employee from filing a timely charge. Once an employee receives unambiguous notification of a discriminatory act, the statute of limitations begins to run. An employee's optimistic belief that his employment might continue, or an application for a different position goes unrewarded, does not change the date of the original discriminatory act.

Likewise, the date that a plant closes is not the date of a discriminatory act if the employee was earlier informed of the closing. The time begins to run the day the employee is notified of the future shutdown.

In limited situations, the date the period begins running may be delayed. Courts have held that the time will begin to run for a rejected applicant when

99

he actually learns the identity of the person selected. In this situation, however, the unsuccessful applicant would be required to show that he had no reasonable way of discovering the identity of the person selected at an earlier date. Failure to inquire would not toll the limitations period.

In like manner, if an employer misleads an applicant who was hired, or misrepresents the reasons why the person was hired, the statute could be equitably tolled to give the applicant additional time to file a charge.

An individual's state of mind, however, is rarely accepted as an excuse for failing to file a timely charge. The time does not run if a person becomes mentally incompetent or institutionalized. Severe depression or personal problems, however, even if caused by the employer's discriminatory act, will not lengthen the statutory period without proof that the individual was rendered incapable of filing a complaint.

In many employment situations involving a discharge, severance payments are made to employees as part of a transition period. The fear of losing a severance payment, or the fear of losing a remaining period of employment, will not normally toll the statute unless the severance agreement illegally restricts the right of an employee to file a charge with the EEOC. While a severance agreement may require an employee to forfeit the right to file a lawsuit, it may not restrict the employee from filing a charge or assisting with an EEOC investigation.

Example:

John Laborer receives a company memorandum on January 1 which states that a major plant reorganization will begin on February 2. On March 3, he is verbally notified of his termination, to begin on June 4. On April 5, he receives written notification of his termination. On May 6, Laborer applies for another job with the company. On June 4, he is discharged. On July 7, he receives his last paycheck.

John Laborer's statute of limitations for an alleged discriminatory discharge began running March 3.

TITLE VII

Title VII is the most unforgiving of statutes for statute of limitations purposes. An employee must file his complaint within either 180 or 300 days of a discriminatory act or be forever barred from raising the claim. Unlike the ADEA, in which the EEOC can file a lawsuit on behalf of an individual without a timely-filed charge, Title VII prohibits the EEOC from filing an agency lawsuit unless an individual has previously filed a charge within the limitations period.

The 180-day deadline applies in states which do not have "deferral agencies." These state or local agencies are empowered to enforce similar charges under state employment discrimination laws. If no deferral agency is available, a claimant must file a charge with the EEOC within 180 days of receiving notice of a discriminatory act.

Most states do have deferral agencies, which extend the limitations period to 300 days. Unless a state agency waives its right to process a claim, Title VII requires the EEOC to allow a state agency 60 days of exclusive jurisdiction. Most state agencies waive their jurisdictional rights after 90, 120 or 180 days following a discriminatory act, however, allowing the EEOC to immediately process a complaint. To insure that the EEOC retains jurisdiction, a complaint should be filed within 240 days of a discriminatory act.

Once a complaint is timely filed under Title VII, an individual is protected against a statute of limitations violation regarding the filing of a lawsuit. When the EEOC completes its investigation, it will contact the complainant with its determination. If no violation is found, the EEOC will provide the complainant with a 90-day notice of a right to sue. A private lawsuit must then be filed in either state or federal court within 90 days from receipt of the notice or the private action will be lost.

It should be noted that a complainant may request a right-to-sue letter from the EEOC at any time after filing a charge. The EEOC must comply with this request

180 days after the charge is filed and may issue the notice at its discretion prior to this time. Once the EEOC issues this notice, however, it will administratively close a file and cease further investigation. Unless a complainant has the ability, both financial and legal, to litigate the claim himself, a right-to-sue request should not be made. It is very difficult for such a request to be rescinded if problems are encountered at a later time.

ADEA

The importance of filing a timely charge with the EEOC is to protect an individual's right to file a private lawsuit even if the EEOC disagrees that a discriminatory act has occurred. Under the ADEA, an individual must file a charge with the EEOC within 180 days of the alleged discriminatory act if there is no state or local agency with which he can file a charge. If a state or locality does maintain an agency which protects against age discrimination, a charge may be filed with the EEOC within 300 days of an unlawful act. A person who does not file within the 180/300-day deadline may not file a lawsuit in federal court without the EEOC filing on his behalf.

Unlike Title VII, a person who misses the 180/300-day deadline may still file a charge with the EEOC up to three years after the date of a discriminatory act. While Title VII requires a timely-filed charge within the 180/300-day deadline, the ADEA allows the EEOC to file a lawsuit on an individual's behalf without a timely-filed charge, so long as the EEOC acts within three years. Because of the time required for an EEOC investigation, however, it is strongly recommended that an individual file with the agency well before the two- or three-year statute of limitations.

Once a charge is timely filed, the next date of importance is two years after the discriminatory act. Under the ADEA, a **lawsuit** must be filed within this two-year period, whether the EEOC has made a final determination on the original charge or not. This limitation is lengthened to three years if a "willful" violation is shown. Willful violations are not easy to prove, however, as will be discussed in a later section. Although other violations, such as the failure to display an EEOC poster, may extend the limitations period, a lawsuit should be filed within two years of the discriminatory act if at all possible.

Willful Violations

The statute of limitations for filing a lawsuit under the ADEA is two years from the discriminatory act, or three years for a suit arising out of a willful violation. As defined by the Supreme Court most recently in **McLaughlin v. Richland Shoe Co.,** 108 S. Ct. 1677 (1988), the term "willful" means that "the employer either knew or showed reckless disregard for the matter of whether its conduct was prohibited by the statute." If an employer acts reasonably in determining its legal obligation, then its action will not be viewed as willful. The willful violation section under "Damages" provides a more detailed discussion of this standard.

Age Discrimination Claims Assistance Act of 1988

On April 7, 1988, President Ronald Reagan signed into law the Age Discrimination Claims Assistance Act of 1988 (Assistance Act). The Assistance Act was enacted in response to the EEOC's failure to process over 2,000 ADEA charges before the running of the statute of limitations. As a result, many individuals who filed charges lost their right to file private lawsuits.

The Assistance Act extends the time for filing an ADEA lawsuit to 540 days from the date of enactment of the law, or September 28, 1989. Four criteria must be met before the Assistance Act applies. First, an ADEA charge must have been timely filed with the EEOC after December 31, 1983. The Commission must not have, within the statute of limitations, either conciliated the matter or notified the person filing the charge of the disposition of the charge and the right to bring a lawsuit. The statute of limitations must have run before the enactment of the Assistance Act, that is, April 7, 1988. Finally, neither the EEOC nor the person with a claim must have filed a lawsuit before the running of the statute of limitations.

Under the Assistance Act, the EEOC was required to notify each person meeting the criteria of the statute of the date on which the new statute of limitations will run and the right of the individual to file suit prior to that date. Individuals who believe that they fall under the statute, but have not been notified, should contact their local EEOC office.

EPA

There is no requirement that an individual file a charge with the EEOC prior to filing a private lawsuit. For individuals desiring to file a lawsuit on their own behalf, the only requirement is that they do so within two years from the last deficient paycheck. This limitations period will expand to three years for willful violations.

For economic reasons, however, most employees prefer the EEOC to process their complaints. An EPA charge may be filed with the Commission at any time prior to the two or three year statute of limitations. Because of the time required to process a complaint, it should be filed as soon as possible after the discriminatory act. Complainants who file their charges one year or more after a violation run a significant risk of the EEOC not completing its investigation prior to the running of the two year limit.

Unlike Title VII, there is no requirement that EPA complainants be disclosed to the employer. The policy of the EEOC is not to identify individuals who file EPA complaints. An employer usually will acquire knowledge about an employee who files a complaint, however, from the type of questions presented by the Commission and the direction of the investigation. Nothing in the Act prevents organizations such as the National Organization for Women from filing a complaint on an individual's behalf.

EXTENDING THE STATUTE OF LIMITATIONS

Continuing Violations

Although not encountered often, some discriminatory acts by an employer are so closely related to prior discriminatory acts that they are considered one event. These "continuing violations" are primarily alleged by employees to make untimely charges timely. For instance, if an employee is denied a promotion because of his race, but fails to file a claim within 300 days of the act, he will be barred from filing a lawsuit. If the same employee is discriminatorily denied a second promotion, however, a timely filed second complaint may be able to incorporate the first failure to be promoted using the continuing violation theory.

Before a court will accept this theory, the discriminatory actions of an employer must be linked by some common thread of evidence. In the promotion scenario above, a common link between the two promotions could be that the same supervisor made both decisions. The employee's second rejection also might have resulted from a discriminatory memorandum placed in the employee's file during the initial discriminatory rejection. Many scenarios are possible, but some type of evidence is required to relate separate acts to a pattern of discrimination.

A second requirement of the continuing violation theory is that both events actually violate a law. In the landmark case of **United Air Lines, Inc. v. Evans,** 431 U.S. 553, 97 S. Ct. 1885 (1977), the United States Supreme Court held that an airline flight attendant who suffered a discriminatory layoff was not entitled to retroactive seniority when later rehired. The stewardess had failed to file a charge within 300 days of her termination, but had filed a timely charge at the time of rehire. Although her termination violated Title VII, the Supreme Court held that the seniority system, in and of itself, did not violate Title VII. Seniority was not bridged for any break in service, whether discriminatory or not. Since both acts did not violate Title VII, the continuing violation theory was rejected.

The continuing violation theory is still under development. As a rule of thumb, however, acts alleged to fall within its parameters probably need to be instigated by the same decision maker. It also is helpful if both acts fall within the same category, such as salary, demotions, promotions or harassment. Once the theory is accepted, however, the time for filing a charge of discrimination runs anew each day that the discriminatory practice continues.

Poster Requirement

Title VII and the ADEA require every employer to post conspicuously at all times a notice prepared or approved by the EEOC setting forth excerpts from or summaries of the Acts and information pertinent to filing a complaint. The purpose of the notice requirement is to alert employees to their federal rights.

The failure of an employer to post a conspicuous notice will extend the amount of time an employee has to file a charge of discrimination with the EEOC. Where an employee usually has 180/300 days to file his charge, additional days can be added for each day a federal poster is not in full view.

Courts differ on the length of the extension. Some courts toll the statute until the employee has acquired general knowledge of his rights or acquired the means to obtain the knowledge. Other courts look to when the employee actually knew his rights. In the former situation, tolling would not be appropriate once the employee consulted with an attorney, since he would have had the opportunity to learn of his rights.

The period will not be tolled if the employer has conspicuously posted the notice even if the employee does not see the notice or sees it and does not become aware of his rights. Posting in a single location may be sufficient if it is centrally located and employees are likely to pass it. In asserting that he did not see the notice or that the employer did not post one, the employee must state in specific detail that he looked but did not see a notice.

If no notice is posted, the burden is on the employer

to prove that the employee is aware of his rights. If the employee is an attorney or performs many of the employer's personnel duties, the period will not be tolled even if no notice is posted, because the employee is considered to know his rights.

Under Title VII, an employer is also subject to a $100 fine for each failure to post notice that is found to be a willful violation of the posting requirement.

VI.

Damages

TITLE VII AND ADEA

The primary goal of Title VII and the ADEA is to put a person who has been discriminated against in the position that he would have been in had the employer not discriminated, that is, to make the employee "whole." There are three types of remedies available to the employee. One remedy is damages. Damages include wages the employee would have earned had the employer not discriminated and any benefits the employee would have received. Second, the employee may be entitled to employment, if the employee was not hired; reinstatement, if the employee was discharged; or promotion, if the employee was not promoted. Finally, for willful violations under the ADEA, the employee may be awarded liquidated or "double" damages.

The time period for damages is divided into a back pay and a front pay period. The back pay period begins when the alleged discriminatory act occurs and ends at the date of trial. The front pay period begins at the date of trial and runs into the future. To calculate the amount of back pay, an employee will initially add the amounts of salary and other payments and benefits, including increased pension benefits, the employee would have received in the job sought. If the employee can show he would have received raises or commissions during the period, these would also be included in the amount of back pay. The employee may also include any cost to him for benefits which the employer would have paid during employment, such as medical bills or insurance premiums.

The law places a duty on an employee to mitigate or lessen his damages, however. Therefore, the salary received from other employment will be deducted from the back pay calculation. Even if the employee did not find another job, any amount which the employee could have earned through reasonable diligence is deducted. If the employee looked diligently for other employment but found none, no deduction would be made.

If an employee thereafter finds two separate jobs, one full-time and one part-time, the salary from the part-time job would not be deducted.

An employer can stop the running of a back pay period by making the employee an unconditional, good faith offer of reinstatement to the same or similar position prior to the date of trial. This is true whether the employee accepts or rejects the offer. The employee may not condition his acceptance on the employer furnishing the back pay at issue or admitting liability.

Certain payments are also deducted from a damage award. If the employee received severance pay after a discharge, the amount of severance will be deducted. This severance is deductible only if it represents a payment the employee would not have received had the employer not discharged the employee. Regular pension payments to which the employee was already entitled are not deductible.

Social security benefits or unemployment compensation is not deductible from damages.

Despite what may be seen on **LA Law** or other television series, Title VII and the ADEA are not get-rich statutes. Damages for emotional distress or pain and suffering are not recoverable under either statute.

Reinstatement is a preferred remedy for cases in which an employer discharges an employee in violation of Title VII or the ADEA. Courts will decide whether reinstatement is appropriate on a case-by-case basis. The judge must consider carefully the facts of the case including the relationship between the employer and employee and whether a comparable position is available. The judge will also look to whether there is excessive hostility or animosity between the parties. If the relationship has deteriorated or is poisoned to the extent that it is unlikely the employer and employee can work cooperatively, reinstatement would be inappropriate. In such a case, front pay or future damages would be substituted for reinstatement. Front pay typically will be ordered for five years or less.

Finally, if an employer is found to have willfully violated the ADEA, the employee is entitled to liquidated damages. Liquidated damages equal the amount of back pay damages and, therefore, are sometimes called double damages.

Willful Violations

A successful claimant under the ADEA may recover double the amount of actual damages if he can prove the violation was "willful." There is no possibility of such double or "liquidated" damages under Title VII.

Until recently, there had been a controversy as to the exact definition courts should apply to the willfulness requirement. For a number of years after the enactment of the ADEA, the standard applied to prove willfulness was an "in the picture" standard. Basically, if the facts of a case were such that an employer would be on notice that the ADEA might be involved, the "in the picture" standard would apply. This was usually proven by showing that the employer was aware of the ADEA and violated it nonetheless.

As the years passed, however, it became almost impossible for an employer to state that it was unaware of the ADEA. Under such a lenient standard, nearly every violation became a willful violation subject to liquidated damages. Because the intent of the liquidated damages provisions is to penalize especially egregious conduct, the United States Supreme Court in **Trans World Airlines, Inc. v. Thurston,** 469 U.S. 111 (1985), adopted a standard of "knowing or reckless disregard" before double damages could be awarded in ADEA cases. Under this stricter standard, an employee must not only show that an employer violated the ADEA, but that it did so under circumstances in which a reasonable person would have known he was violating the ADEA.

In at least one circuit, double damages will not be awarded unless there is "outrageous conduct" in addition to activity displaying knowing and reckless disregard for the ADEA. Examples of outrageous conduct include termination of an employee shortly before his pension vests, the systematic removal of older employees or evidence that the employer had previously violated discrimination statutes. In every circuit, however, showing that the employer acted with knowing or reckless disregard of the ADEA will add a third year to the statute of limitations. There is no requirement that outrageous conduct be shown to increase the statute of limitations by the one additional year.

While "knowing" conduct probably requires some type of direct evidence that the employer acted for discriminatory reasons, there is no clear definition of what constitutes "reckless disregard" under the ADEA. What may be reckless disregard to one jury may not even prove a violation before another. Certainly some type of outrageous or egregious conduct will improve a claimant's ability to prove a willful violation. An employer, on the other hand, will most likely be able to protect itself against findings of willful conduct if it checks with its legal department or advisors prior to instituting an employment action. The mere seeking of legal advice shows an institutional concern for compliance with the Act.

EPA

Successful claimants always recover back wages making their salaries equal to those of employees of the opposite sex. What is very significant, however, is the requirement that prevailing plaintiffs also receive an equal amount of unpaid wages as liquidated damages. It is the "substantial burden" of the employer to prove that it should not be penalized by double damages.

To avoid liquidated damages, an employer must show that the act or omission giving rise to a lawsuit was made in good faith and that the employer had reasonable grounds for believing that it did not violate the EPA. An employer will not meet this burden merely by stating that it was unaware of the violation. It must produce evidence that it had honest intentions in ascertaining and following the EPA requirements. Requesting legal advice prior to the setting of salaries would be the type of evidence which could persuade a court that it would be unfair to impose more than a compensatory damage award.

Unlike Title VII, in which no liquidated damages are possible, and the ADEA, which requires an employer's gross negligence, a plaintiff under the EPA will likely receive an increased award. If for this reason alone, a person with a sex-wage discrimination complaint should file under both the EPA and Title VII.

VII.
EEOC Administrative Process

The most frequent complaint heard from individuals utilizing the EEOC's administrative process is the length of time required to complete an investigation. Without a doubt, the process can and will test a complainant's patience. To insure that the investigation takes the shortest time possible, a complainant should prepare his case to the greatest extent prior to filing an EEOC charge.

The first step for an employee who believes that he is the victim of a discriminatory act is to locate the closest EEOC or state employment discrimination agency. A complaint can usually be filed with both agencies at either location. Only one agency will actually investigate the charge, however, subject to review by the second agency after a decision is rendered. A complainant may choose the agency he desires to investigate the charge. If the complainant does not state a preference, however, the agency that processes the complaint typically will conduct the investigation.

It is important that a charge be filed as close to the date of the discriminatory act as possible. The statute of limitations on many claims is two years from the discriminatory act and an agency may need all of that time to complete its investigation. Even if a statute of limitations does not appear to affect a case, memories of witnesses often fade with time. The quicker a charge is filed, the quicker the investigation will be completed.

A complainant who enters an EEOC office will

be handed a questionnaire to fill out in the office. The questionnaire asks basic information, such as the name and address of the complainant, and facts upon which the case is based. The questionnaire will be taken to an EEOC investigator assigned to intake duties, who will collect the papers required to file a charge under the particular statute involved. The investigator will then meet with the complainant to discuss the facts of the case in greater detail.

Although a complainant is not required to provide sufficient facts to prove his case at the intake stage, he must provide some evidence of discriminatory treatment. A complainant who bases his claim on the fact that he was fired and is black will be asked for additional information, such as the names of white employees in similar circumstances who were not discharged. A complainant without additional information will be told that there is no basis for a written complaint. Although every individual has the right to file a charge, whether or not a basis for the charge has been established, a charge without some evidence of discriminatory treatment will be administratively closed without investigation.

It is important for an individual to bring as much information as possible to the initial meeting. Although most complainants fail to compile such information, an investigation will get off to a quicker start if the complainant can provide witness names and phone numbers, along with salary information and other forms of documentation relevant to the charge, such as evaluations and job descriptions.

Once the case is discussed with an investigator, the investigator will prepare a charge for signature. A complainant should anticipate from two to four hours to file a complaint. If a complainant cannot, for example, take off enough time from work to complete a charge, a complaint may be mailed to the individual for signing. Mistakes have occurred in this situation, however, which will delay an investigation. It is recommended that an individual complete the process as early as possible, preferably at the first meeting.

The signed charge will be assigned to an investigator, usually within one month. The assignment may or may not be with the intake investigator who processed the charge. The investigator who receives the assignment will contact the complainant by telephone or mail. A complainant therefore should be diligent in keeping the agency abreast of any changes of address. A complainant that does not receive notice within three months of filing a charge that his case has been assigned to an investigator should contact the EEOC to insure that the charge was not mishandled.

The investigator will begin the investigation by sending a questionnaire to the employer. Most questions will request information about other employees in the same or similar circumstances as the complainant. In most cases, the employer will be given one month to respond. Typically, an employer will request and be granted extensions to answer the questions. Follow-up questionnaires will be sent out as required.

Although investigators do not have time to engage in detailed discussions every time that a complainant calls, an investigator should be contacted every four months or so to inquire into the investigation's progress. Many times an individual will be able to clarify responses made by an employer.

It is important to remember that an investigator is a neutral party at this stage of the investigation. Many complainants are under the mistaken impression that an investigator represents the charging party during the investigatory stage. An investigator has the responsibility to remain neutral, however, until a cause finding is actually made in a case. Prior to that time, the investigator represents the public interest, which includes the employer under investigation.

Upon completion of an investigation, the investigator will recommend a "cause" or "no cause" determination, subject to review by a supervisor. A cause finding means there is reasonable cause to believe a violation has occurred. No cause findings result in a complaint being administratively closed. Cause findings are then forwarded to a district legal unit to be reviewed by a Commission attorney. The attorney either will approve the cause finding, at which point a letter of determination is mailed to the employer announcing the finding, recommend a no cause finding or request the investigator to obtain additional information.

Once a cause finding is issued, the EEOC is required under the ADEA and Title VII to attempt conciliation with the employer. At this stage, the EEOC investigator involved in the conciliation process typically will request close to full relief with regard to back pay and reinstatement.

Should conciliation fail, the file will be returned to the district legal unit which originally approved the cause finding. An attorney will write a report, called a "presentation memorandum" which explains the facts of the case and recommends for or against litigation. The presentation memorandum is sent to the five EEOC commissioners in Washington, D.C. If three of the commissioners vote to approve litigation, a lawsuit will be filed in federal district court by the Commission's district office.

The administrative process has a number of steps from the filing of a charge to the possible filing of a lawsuit. A complainant who is confused by the process should not hesitate to call the EEOC for clarification. Each district office has an attorney on call to answer questions from the public. Individuals who desire to discuss their case prior to the filing of a charge should call their district office and request to speak with the "attorney-of-the-day." After a charge is filed, the investigator assigned to the case is the chief source of information for a complainant with a question.

VIII.
Procedures for Federal Employees

Federal employees who believe they are the victims of discrimination have a different set of procedural requirements than their private sector counterparts. Although the analysis is identical for determining whether discrimination has occurred, a federal employee has different time limitations and filing locations when seeking redress for adverse employment actions.

A federal employee must initially consult with an Equal Employment Opportunity (EEO) counselor at his agency within 30 days after receiving notice of a discriminatory act or within 30 days after an adverse personnel action actually occurs. Therefore, an employee who receives notice that he will be discharged in three months may seek redress at two separate times: (1) after receiving the notice; and (2) within 30 days of the actual discharge.

A formal complaint is not filed with the EEO counselor at the initial meeting. The counselor will take the employee's statement and contact agency supervisors regarding the facts of the case. At this point, an effort will be made to resolve the problems without resorting to formal proceedings.

If the complaint cannot be informally resolved, however, the employee will receive written notice that the counselor will take no further actions. An employee has 15 days from receipt of this notice to file a formal complaint with the agency in question. It should be noted that an employee may file a formal complaint prior to receiving an EEO counselor's written

119

notice if a settlement is not reached within 21 days of the first informal consultation with the counselor.

Once an employee files a formal complaint, the agency can either accept or reject it. If the agency rejects it, the employee has a right of appeal, which is discussed later in the chapter. Most complaints will be accepted, however, setting the administrative process in motion.

The complaint will be assigned to an investigator, who will gather evidence relating to the matter. In most cases, the evidence will include written statements from the employee, supervisors and co-workers with knowledge of events leading to the complaint. Personnel files, evaluations and other documents will be collected. Once the investigation is complete, a copy of the file will be provided to the complainant.

Settlement negotiations typically occur at this time. At any point in the process settlement discussions may be held, but the case is more easily evaluated at the completion of the investigation. This is also the final stage before an administrative hearing is held.

If a settlement is not reached, an agency will provide the employee with written notice of its proposed findings. This document will also inform the employee of his right to demand a hearing. The employee has 15 days after receipt of the findings to demand a hearing. The employee will invariably request a hearing, since the agency's proposed findings become final if such a request is not made.

Administrative hearings are conducted by EEOC hearings examiners. The examiners are comprised of attorneys trained in employment law. The hearing itself resembles an informal courtroom trial. Witnesses provide testimony under oath, including cross-examination, and documents are placed into evidence. At the completion of the hearings, the examiner will make his findings and determination.

Although a hearing examiner's determination is advisory in nature, most findings will ultimately be enacted. Both parties, however, have a right to appeal a decision. If an agency believes a holding for an employee was made in error, it can modify or reject the decision. An employee, in that circumstance, would appeal the agency's modification or rejection to the EEOC's Office of Review and Appeals (ORA). If the original holding was unfavorable to an employee, the employee may also appeal to the ORA. Employees have 20 days after receipt of the agency's notice of final decision to file a notice of appeal.

ORA will review the complaint file, documentary evidence and hearing transcript prior to making its decision. Its determination is binding on an agency. If ORA finds for the employee, it requires the agency to provide it with written notification of the steps taken to correct the situation. ORA then monitors the agency until full compliance is achieved.

AGE DISCRIMINATION

Federal employees alleging age discrimination have the right to file a lawsuit in federal court after first giving the EEOC 30 days' notice of an intent to file suit. The adverse employment action must have occurred within 180 days of the notice.

EQUAL PAY DISCRIMINATION

Federal employees alleging sex-based equal pay violations must file their complaint with an EEOC field office instead of the employing agency.

FILING A LAWSUIT

A federal employee is authorized to file a lawsuit in United States district court when one of the following requirements is met:

(a) Within 30 days or receipt of notice of final action taken by the agency on a complaint;

(b) After 180 days from the date of filing a

complaint with the agency if there has been
no decision;
(c) Within 30 days after receipt of notice of final
action taken by the EEOC on an appeal; or
(d) After 180 days after the date of filing an appeal
with the EEOC if there has been no Commission
decision.

IX.
Preventing Charges
of Discrimination

No system has been devised, or can be devised, which will prevent every employee complaint of employment discrimination. The identity of most individuals is so closely related to their employment status that any adverse action relating to quality of performance is regarded as a personal attack. Most employees believe they are doing a good job, or at least as good a job as their co-workers, and, therefore, regard most criticism as unjustified.

The purpose of this chapter is not to prevent all discrimination complaints, but to create a personnel system in which problems can be managed as quickly and inexpensively as possible. Some of the ideas may actually increase the number of internal complaints in the short-term, but decrease the amount of external litigation in the long-term. This trade-off reduces costs not only in terms of dollar expenditures, but also in terms of inconvenience and company resources required to defend discrimination lawsuits.

A strong internal policing system also should result in an increase in employee productivity. Employees who are confident that grievances will be investigated in a thorough and fair manner are more likely to discuss problems in the open, instead of allowing problems to affect work habits for months or years.

A recurring theme of this chapter is paperwork. Even though a supervisor may be available to testify at trial or provide an affidavit in response to an EEOC interrogatory, information provided after an employee has filed a complaint is tainted by a self-serving motivation. Paperwork created prior to a charge, however, may be challenged for correctness but will often pass a test of sincerity. A business has the right to make poor decisions as long as it does not make those decisions based on race, age, sex, religion or national origin.

APPLICATIONS

Although not statutorily prohibited, many employers have removed the date of birth and graduation entries from their application forms. One defense to an age complaint is the lack of knowledge that an applicant is within the protected age group. Similar steps can also be taken to remove race-related questions.

INTERVIEWS

A determination of objectives prior to a series of interviews is advisable from both a business and discrimination standpoint. By first determining the objectives of an interview, it is easier to create a list of standard questions to be asked each candidate. It is important that every applicant be asked the same core of questions used to judge other applicants. Employers who do not ask each applicant the same questions leave themselves open to the charge that certain candidates were not taken seriously. An employer who asks a 50-year-old candidate more general questions than asked younger counterparts gives the appearance of having eliminated the 50-year-old because of age, not skill. Even if the initial answers in an interview tend to show that a candidate will probably not be selected, the same core questions should still be completed.

In the same vein, small talk should be kept to a minimum. Many employment consultants recommend opening an interview with a friendly question to relax an applicant. After a brief introduction, however, the questions should be relatively structured. Interviews without purpose not only expose an employer to charges that it did not take an applicant seriously, but also provide an interviewer with a greater opportunity of making a statement which could be construed as discriminatory. While it is impossible to script an interview verbatim, an employer that grades candidates on specific questions and answers will have a better chance of successfully defending a charge based on an inadvertent interview statement.

Interviewers must be aware of the wording they use during an interview. Especially in age cases, statements regarding birthdates, length of employment, etc. are easily construed as discriminatory by applicants very cognizant of age. Interviewers should be counselled to leave personal prejudices at home, where they will not be construed as the employer's.

The standard set of questions eventually asked the candidates should lend themselves to objective measurement to the greatest extent possible. One benefit of setting objectives prior to an interview is that interviewers will know what to look for in an applicant's answer. In an effort to hire the best employee instead of best interviewer, questions involving past work behavior often lead to answers which are more easily compared. For a position as a Congressional assistant, for example, a question posed as "When faced with an impossible deadline on your last job, what did you do?" will provide a more easily compared answer than "How do you work under pressure?"

Interviewers must take thorough notes. Since it is not always possible to write everything down during an interview, time should be budgeted between interviews to complete the interview notes. Again, wording should be checked for possible discriminatory connotations.

Applicants that receive thorough professional interviews will likely believe that they received a fair opportunity to be hired. A thorough paper trail of pre-interview objectives and post-interview notes will place an employer in the best position to defend charges alleging otherwise.

EVALUATIONS

No aspect of employment law breeds more litigation than evaluations which lack honesty or detail. Whether because of fear of alienation, confrontation or other reasons, many employers rate average employees as good or outstanding. The fear of confrontation today, however, can create hostile and often losing confrontation years later.

Evaluation inflation has proven particularly significant during the past decade when many companies and organizations consolidated their workforces. The typical ADEA complainant is a white mid-level manager in his 50's who is a victim of a company reduction-in-force. Many of these managers have evaluations showing long-term exemplary work. Statements by supervisors that they actually were average performers usually appear self-serving after a charge is filed.

The first step for an employer is to conduct a study of its evaluation system. A typical five-point system should have few outstandings, some goods and a majority of averages (the final two categories being below average and poor). An employer which determines that it has evaluation inflation should change the policy as soon as possible. A memorandum can explain to employees that the evaluation system is being revised and that a lower score on the next evaluation may not necessarily mean worsened performance. It also should be explained that average evaluations are not considered unsatisfactory performance.

In approximately two or three years the evaluation system will again become functional for reduction-in-force purposes. It should be noted that an employer should attempt to revise its evaluation system well before a reduction-in-force is contemplated. In the midst of massive layoffs, a change in the evaluation system will be greeted with skepticism.

In addition to honest evaluations, there is a need for detail. While objective evaluations based on measured performance are the easiest to defend, even subjective categories such as initiative, creativity and attitude can be supported through detailed explanations of performance. Detail is particularly important when an employee with consistent ratings is being downgraded. This can be especially helpful if employees are allowed to read and sign their evaluations. Even when an employee disagrees with a grading, a signed evaluation will have far more credibility with an EEOC investigator or a jury.

Although often subjective in nature, employers should also consider ranking the employees in their workforce on a yearly basis. The ranking should clearly state that it is being made on a performance basis only. Rankings based on potential or promotability may impact on older employees and actually be used as evidence of an employer's discriminatory intent. Employers should thereafter insure that older employees are not always ranked below younger counterparts. Obviously, the rankings should be consistent with the overall evaluation ratings, i.e., employees rated outstanding on top, then good, average, etc. Rankings made years prior to a required employment decision are often regarded as an employer's unbiased opinion.

EARLY RETIREMENT PLANS AND WAIVER/RELEASES

Early retirement plans are not evidence of discrimination if the plans are offered on a voluntary basis. As long as the employee has the right to remain employed, or be considered for employment in a reduction-in-force situation, an offer of early retirement cannot be used against the employer without further evidence of discriminatory intent. This is true even if an older employee who voluntarily retired is replaced by a younger employee.

In return for benefits provided in an early retirement plan, an employer typically will seek a waiver or release of employment discrimination claims from a retiring individual. In other words, an employee will receive increased benefits for agreeing not to file a lawsuit against the employer. Clearly, the benefits offered must be greater than those to which the employee is already entitled. In the same vein, an employer may not require an employee to sign a waiver to receive severance pay other employees receive without signing a waiver.

For releases to be enforceable, certain elements must be present in an agreement. According to the EEOC, an employee must enter into a release in a knowing and voluntary manner. To be considered knowing and voluntary, four elements must be present: (1) The employee has a sufficient amount of time to consider the agreement. Although there is no specific minimum time period, an employer should provide an employee at least 30 days to consider it; (2) The release should advise an employee to consult an attorney; (3) The ADEA, Title VII and any other statute involved should be mentioned by name in the agreement. A contract releasing "all claims" of an employee may be considered insufficient notice of the particular rights an employee is waiving; (4) An employee has the right to negotiate and have input into the terms of an agreement. Although this requirement is not settled law, settlement agreements in which the employee has participated are more likely to be considered voluntary than agreements offered by employers on a "take it or leave it" basis.

Agreements should be drafted in clear and simple language. Language which is not clear will be interpreted against the author of the document, in this case, the employer.

SEXUAL HARASSMENT POLICIES

Sexual harassment complaints must be taken seriously not only because of the sharp increase in the number of complaints in the past few years but also because of the potential liability facing a corporation charged with sexual harassment. Sexual harassment complaints, particularly those involving incidents of sexual intercourse, often combine state civil claims with Title VII claims. State claims, typically including assault and the intentional infliction of emotional distress, often allow a plaintiff to recover punitive and pain and suffering damages which far exceed the actual monetary loss recoverable under Title VII. An aggressive policy of investigation and discipline offers employers the greatest amount of protection. An employer becomes liable for the actions of its employees only when it knows or should have known of the prohibited acts. Therefore, it is important that an employer encourage internal complaints of sexual harassment so that problems may be corrected prior to incurring substantial legal liability.

A company should have a written policy which specifically states that sexual harassment will not be tolerated. The document should be written in plain and simple terms and state with specificity the types of activity prohibited. A good place to start is to incorporate the EEOC Guidelines which prohibit: (1) employees being led to believe they will lose their jobs if they fail to submit to sexual overtures; (2) the loss of a promotion or good work assignment for an employee who fails to submit to sexual overtures; and (3) sexual conduct which interferes with an employee's performance or creates a hostile or offensive work environment. A hostile environment should be further defined to include vulgar or offensive jokes, as well as demeaning graffiti, posters and calendars.

A mere memo, however, will not insulate an employer unless it is willing to back up the policy with actions. An employer must establish a system in which employees notify company officials of sexual harassment without the fear of retaliation. Therefore, a complainant should be provided confidentiality to every extent possible during an investigation. Supervisors should be instructed that even if a sexual harassment complaint is not substantiated, adverse employment actions will not be tolerated.

The system itself should provide the names of two separate individuals in two separate departments where acts of harassment can be reported. Employees are not required to report acts of sexual harassment to the individuals instigating the harassment. Therefore,

it is critical that a policy not require an employee
to report such incidents to her immediate supervisor.
In a majority of cases, an allegation will contend that
a supervisor is requesting sexual favors from a subordinate. By designating two separate employees (it is
suggested that at least one employee be a female
to prevent an allegation that trauma from the incident
would not allow a person to complain to a member
of the opposite sex) in two different departments,
an employee would always have the opportunity to
complain to an individual outside of her immediate
line of authority.

Some employees will never be impressed by a
memorandum. It is strongly suggested, therefore,
that the employees be given a short seminar stressing
the company policy and seriousness of the issue. Individuals may take the issue more seriously when the
personal ramifications are explained. In many cases
of sexual harassment, the individual as well as the
employer is sued and subject to large monetary judgments. A loss of money and employment may catch
their attention.

Each employee should be required to sign his name
signifying attendance at a seminar. Likewise, employees
should be required to initial their receipt of the employer's written policy regarding sexual harassment.
This will protect an employer against claims alleging
months or years of sexual harassment. In such circumstances, an employee will be hard-pressed to explain
why she did not seek help for her problems when they
first occurred.

A policy is only words, however, unless it is backed
up by action. Complaints of sexual harassment must
be immediately and thoroughly investigated. Juries
take incidents of sexual harassment seriously, and
corporations which delay investigating these claims
leave themselves open to large damage awards. Investigations should be conducted by employees outside
the division in question, preferably by the legal or
EEO department. Prompt corrective action often will
shield an employer from liability even when an offensive
action is found to have occurred. When an employer

does find a violation, it should use the same disciplinary system that is in place for other violations of company policy.

The major thrust of the suggestions is to increase internal complaints in the present, which will decrease external complaints in the future. When employees realize that sexual harassment will not be tolerated, however, incidents of sexual harassment will decrease, and employee productivity will improve.

Appendix A
Title VII of the Civil Rights Act of 1964, as Amended

An Act

To enforce the constitutional right to vote, to confer jurisdiction upon the district courts of the United States to provide injunctive relief against discrimination in public accommodations, to authorize the Attorney General to institute suits to protect constitutional rights in public facilities and public education, to extend the Commission on Civil Rights, to prevent discrimination in federally assisted programs, to establish a Commission on Equal Employment Opportunity, and for other purposes.

Be it enacted by the Senate and House of Representatives of the United States of America in Congress assembled, That this Act may be cited as the "Civil Rights Act of 1964".

Title VII—Equal Employment Opportunity

Definitions

SEC. 701. For the purposes of this Title—
(a) The term "person" includes one or more individuals, governments, governmental agencies, political subdivisions, labor unions, partnerships, associations, corporations, legal representatives, associations, corporations legal representatives, mutual companies, joint-stock companies, trusts, unincorporated organizations, trustees, trustees in bankruptcy, or receivers.

133

(b) The term "employer" means a person engaged in an industry affecting commerce who has fifteen or more employees for each working day in each of twenty or more calendar weeks in the current or preceding calendar year, and any agent of such a person, but such term does not include (1) the United States, a corporation wholly owned by the Government of the United States, an Indian tribe, or any department or agency of the District of Columbia subject by statute to procedures of the competitive service (as defined in section 2102 of title 5 of the United States Code), or (2) a bona fide private membership club (other than a labor organization) which is exempt from taxation under section 501(c) of the Internal Revenue Code of 1954, except that during the first year after the date of enactment of the Equal Employment Opportunity Act of 1972, persons having fewer than twenty-five employees (and their agents) shall not be considered employers.

(c) The term "employment agency" means any person regularly undertaking with or without compensation to procure employees for an employer or to procure for employees opportunities to work for an employer and includes an agent of such a person.

(d) The term "labor organization" means a labor organization engaged in an industry affecting commerce, and any agent of such an organization, and includes any organization of any kind, any agency, or employee representation committee, group, association, or plan so engaged in which employees participate and which exists for the purpose, in whole or in part, of dealing with employers concerning grievances, labor disputes, wages, rates of pay, hours, or other terms or conditions of employment, and any conference, general committee, joint or system board, or joint council so engaged which is subordinate to a national or international labor organization.

(e) A labor organization shall be deemed to be engaged in an industry affecting commerce if (1) it maintains or operates a hiring hall or hiring office which procures employees for an employer or procures for employees opportunities to work for an employer, or (2) the number of its members (or, where it is a labor organization composed of other labor organizations or their representatives, if the aggregate number of the members of such other labor organization) is (A) twenty-five or more during the first year after the date of enactment of the Equal Employment Opportunity Act of 1972, or (B) fifteen or more thereafter, and such labor organization—

(1) is the certified representative of employees under

the provisions of the National Labor Relations Act, as
amended, or the Railway Labor Act, as amended;

(2) although not certified, is a national or international
labor organization or a local labor organization recognized
or acting as the representative of employees of an employer
or employers engaged in an industry affecting commerce;
or

(3) has chartered a local labor organization or subsidiary
body which is representing or actively seeking to represent
employees of employers within the meaning of paragraph
(1) or (2); or

(4) has been chartered by a labor organization representing or actively seeking to represent employees within
the meaning of paragraph (1) or (2) as the local or subordinate
body through which such employees may enjoy membership
or become affiliated with such labor organization; or

(5) is a conference, general committee, joint or system
board, or joint council subordinate to a national or international labor organization, which includes a labor organization engaged in an industry affecting commerce within the
meaning of any of the preceding paragraphs of this subsection.

(f) The term "employee" means an individual employed by
an employer, except that the term "employee" shall not
include any person elected to public office in any State
or political subdivision of any State by the qualified voters
thereof, or any person chosen by such officer to be on such
officer's personal staff, or an appointee on the policymaking
level or an immediate advisor with respect to the exercise
of the constitutional or legal powers of the office. The exemption set forth in the preceding sentence shall not include
employees subject to the civil service laws of a State government, governmental agency or political subdivision.

(g) The term "commerce" means trade, traffic, commerce,
transportation, transmission, or communication among the
several States; or between a State and any place outside
thereof; or within the District of Columbia, or a possession
of the United States; or between points in the same State
but through a point outside thereof.

(h) The term "industry affecting commerce" means any
activity, business, or industry in commerce or in which a
labor dispute would hinder or obstruct commerce or the
free flow of commerce and includes any activity or industry
"affecting commerce" within the meaning of the Labor-
Management Reporting and Disclosure Act of 1959, and
further includes any governmental industry, business, or
activity.

(i) The term "State" includes a State of the United States,

the District of Columbia, Puerto Rico, the Virgin Islands, American Samoa, Guam, Wake Island, the Canal Zone, and Outer Continental Shelf lands defined in the Outer Continental Shelf Lands Act.

(j) The term "religion" includes all aspects of religious observance and practice, as well as belief, unless an employer demonstrates that he is unable to reasonably accommodate to an employee's or prospective employee's, religious observance or practice without undue hardship on the conduct of the employer's business.

(k) The terms, "because of sex" or "on the basis of sex" include, but are not limited to, because of or on the basis of pregnancy, childbirth or related medical conditions; and women affected by pregnancy, childbirth, or related medical conditions shall be treated the same for all employment-related purposes, including receipt of benefits under fringe benefit programs, as other persons not so affected but similar in their ability or inability to work, and nothing in section 703(h) of this title shall be interpreted to permit otherwise. This subsection shall not require an employer to pay for health insurance benefits for abortion, except where the life of the mother would be endangered if the fetus were carried to term, or except where medical complications have arisen from an abortion: Provided, That nothing herein shall preclude an employer from providing abortion benefits or otherwise affect bargaining agreements in regard to abortion.

Exemption

SEC. 702. This title shall not apply to an employer with respect to the employment of aliens outside any State, or to a religious corporation, association, educational institution, or society with respect to the employment of individuals of a particular religion to perform work connected with the carrying on by such corporation, association, educational institution, or society of its activities.

Discrimination Because of Race, Color, Religion, Sex, or National Origin

SEC. 703. (a) It shall be an unlawful employment practice for an employer—

(1) to fail or refuse to hire or to discharge any individual, or otherwise to discriminate against any individual with respect to his compensation, terms, conditions, or privileges of employment, because of such individual's race, color, religion, sex, or national origin; or

(2) To limit, segregate, or classify his employees or applicants for employment in any way which would deprive or tend to deprive any individual of employment opportunities or otherwise adversely affect his status as an employee, because of such individual's race, color, religion, sex, or national origin.

(b) It shall be an unlawful employment practice for an employment agency to fail or refuse to refer for employment, or otherwise to discriminate against, any individual because of his race, color, religion, sex, or national origin, or to classify or refer for employment any individual on the basis of his race, color, religion, sex, or national origin.

(c) It shall be an unlawful employment practice for a labor organization—

(1) to exclude or to expel from its membership, or otherwise to discriminate against any individual because of his race, color, religion, sex, or national origin;

(2) to limit, segregate, or classify its membership, or applicants for membership or to classify or fail or refuse to refer for employment any individual, in any way which would deprive or tend to deprive any individual of employment opportunities, or would limit such employment opportunities or otherwise adversely affect his status as an employee or as an applicant for employment, because of such individual's race, color, religion, sex, or national origin; or

(3) to cause or attempt to cause an employer to discriminate against an individual in violation of this section.

(d) It shall be an unlawful employment practice for any employer, labor organization, or joint labor-management committee controlling apprenticeship or other training or retraining, including on-the-job training programs to discriminate against any individual because of his race, color, religion, sex, or national origin in admission to, or employment in, any program established to provide apprenticeship or other training.

(e) Notwithstanding any other provision of this title, (1) it shall not be an unlawful employment practice for an employer to hire and employ employees, for an employment agency to classify, or refer for employment any individual, for a labor organization to classify its membership or to classify or refer for employment any individual, or for an employer, labor organization, or joint labor-management committee controlling apprenticeship or other training or retraining programs to admit or employ any individual in any such program, on the basis of his religion, sex, or national origin in those certain instances where religion, sex, or national origin is a bona fide occupational qualification reasonably necessary to the normal operation of that particular business or enterprise, and (2) it shall not be an unlawful employment practice for a school, college, university, or other educational institution or institution of learning to hire and employ employees of a particular religion if such school, college, university, or other educational institution or institution of learning is, in whole or in substantial part, owned, supported, controlled, or managed by a particular religion or by a particular religious corporation, association, or society, or if the curriculum of such school, college, university, or other educational institution or institution of learning is directed toward the propagation of a particular religion.

(f) As used in this title, the phrase "unlawful employment practice" shall not be deemed to include any action or measure taken by an employer, labor organization, joint labor-management committee, or employment agency with respect to an individual who is a member of the Communist Party of the United States or of any other organization required to register as a Communist-action or Communist-front organization by final order of the Subversive Activities Control Board pursuant to the Subversive Activities Control Act of 1950.

(g) Notwithstanding any other provision of this title, it shall not be an unlawful employment practice for an employer to fail or refuse to hire and employ any individual for any position, for an employer to discharge any individual from any position, or for an employment agency to fail or refuse to refer any individual for employment in any position, or for a labor organization to fail or refuse to refer any individual for employment in any position, if—

(1) the occupancy of such position, or access to the premises in or upon which any part of the duties of such position is performed or is to be performed, is subject to any requirement imposed in the interest of the national security of the United States under any security program in effect pursuant to or administered under any statute of the United States or any Executive Order of the President; and

(2) such individual has not fulfilled or has ceased to fulfill that requirement.

(h) Notwithstanding any other provision of this title, it shall not be an unlawful employment practice for an employer to apply different standards of compensation, or different terms, conditions, or privileges of employment pursuant to a bona fide seniority or merit system, or a system which measures earnings by quantity or quality of production or to employees who work in different locations, provided that such differences are not the result of an intention to discriminate because of race, color, religion, sex, or national origin, or shall it be an unlawful employment practice for an employer to give and to act upon the results of any professionally developed ability test provided that such test, its administration or action upon the results is not designed, intended or used to discriminate because of race, color, religion, sex, or national origin. It shall not be an unlawful employment practice under this title for any employer to differentiate upon the basis of sex in determining the amount of the wages or compensation paid or to be paid to employees of such employer if such differentiation is authorized by the provisions of section 6(d) of the Fair Labor Standards Act of 1938, as amended (29 U.S.C. 206(d)).

(i) Nothing contained in this title shall apply to any business or enterprise on or near an Indian reservation with respect to any publicly announced employment practice of such business or enterprise under which a preferential treatment is given to any individual because he is an Indian living on or near a reservation.

(j) Nothing contained in this title shall be interpreted to require any employer, employment agency, labor organization, or joint labor-management committee subject to this title to grant preferential treatment to any individual or to any group because of the race, color, religion, sex, or national origin of such individual or group on account of an imbalance which may exist with respect to the total number or percentage of persons of any race, color, religion, sex, or national origin employed by any employer, referred or classified for employment by any employment agency or labor organization, admitted to membership or classified by any labor organization, or admitted to, or employed in, any apprenticeship or other training program, in comparison with the total number of percentage of persons of such race, color, religion, sex, or national origin in any community, State, section, or other area, or in the available work force in any community, State, section, or other area.

Other Unlawful Employment Practices

SEC. 704. (a) It shall be an unlawful employment practice for an employer to discriminate against any of his employees or applicants for employment, for an employment agency, or joint labor-management committee controlling apprenticeship or other training or retraining, including on-the-job training programs, to discriminate against any individual, or for a labor organization to discriminate against any member thereof or applicant for membership, because he has opposed

any practice made an unlawful employment practice by
this title, or because he has made a charge, testified, assisted,
or participated in any manner in an investigation, proceeding,
or hearing under this title.

(b) It shall be an unlawful employment practice for an employer, labor organization, employment agency, or joint
labor-management committee controlling apprenticeship
or other training or retraining, including on-the-job training
programs, to print or publish or cause to be printed or published any notice or advertisement relating to employment
by such an employer or membership in or any classification
or referral for employment by such a labor organization,
or relating to any classification or referral for employment
by such an employment agency, or relating to admission
to, or employment in, any program established to provide
apprenticeship or other training by such a joint labor-management committee indicating any preference, limitation, specification, or discrimination, based on race, color, religion,
sex, or national origin, except that such a notice or advertisement may indicate a preference, limitation, specification,
or discrimination based on religion, sex, or national origin
when religion, sex, or national origin is a bona fide occupational qualification for employment.

Equal Employment Opportunity Commission

SEC. 705. (a) There is hereby created a Commission to be
known as the Equal Employment Opportunity Commission,
which shall be composed of five members, not more than
three of whom shall be members of the same political party.
Members of the Commission shall be appointed by the President by and with the advice and consent of the Senate for
a term of five years. Any individual chosen to fill a vacancy
shall be appointed only for the unexpired term of the member
whom he shall succeed, and all members of the Commission
shall continue to serve until their successors are appointed
and qualified, except that no such member of the Commission
shall continue to serve (1) for more than sixty days when the
Congress is in session unless a nomination to fill such vacancy
shall have been submitted to the Senate, or (2) after the
adjournment sine die of the session of the Senate in which
such nomination was submitted. The President shall designate
one member to serve as Chairman of the Commission, and
one member to serve as Vice Chairman. The Chairman
shall be responsible on behalf of the Commission for the
administrative operations of the Commission, and except
as provided in subsection (b), shall appoint, in accordance

with the provisions of title 5, United States Code, governing
appointments in the competitive service, such officers,
agents, attorneys, hearing examiners, and employees as
he deems necessary to assist in the performance of its functions and to fix their compensation in accordance with the
provisions of chapter 51 and subchapter III of chapter 53
of title 5, United States Code, relating to classification
and General Schedule pay rates: Provided, That assignment,
removal, and compensation of hearing examiners shall be
in accordance with sections 3105, 3344, 5362, and 7521 of
title 5, United States Code.

(b) (1) There shall be a General Counsel of the Commission
appointed by the President, by and with the advice and consent
of the Senate, for a term of four years. The General Counsel
shall have responsibility for the conduct of litigation as
provided in sections 706 and 707 of this title. The General
Counsel shall have such other duties as the Commission
may prescribe or as may be provided by law and shall concur
with the Chairman of the Commission on the appointment
and supervision of regional attorneys. The General Counsel
of the Commission on the effective date of this Act shall
continue in such position and perform the functions specified
in this subsection until a successor is appointed and qualified.

(2) Attorneys appointed under this section may, at the
direction of the Commission, appear for and represent the
Commission in any case in court, provided that the Attorney
General shall conduct all litigation to which the Commission
is a party in the Supreme Court pursuant to this title.

(c) A vacancy in the Commission shall not impair the right
of the remaining members to exercise all the powers of
the Commission and three members thereof shall constitute
a quorum.

(d) The Commission shall have an official seal which shall
be judicially noticed.

(e) The Commission shall at the close of each fiscal year
report to the Congress and to the President concerning the
action it has taken; the names, salaries, and duties of all
individuals in its employ and the moneys it has disbursed;
and shall make such further reports on the cause of and
means of eliminating discrimination and such recommendations
for further legislation as may appear desirable.

(f) The principal office of the Commission shall be in or
near the District of Columbia, but it may meet or exercise
any or all of its powers at any other place. The Commission
may establish such regional or State offices as it deems
necessary to accomplish the purpose of this title.

(g) The Commission shall have power—

(1) to cooperate with and, with their consent, utilize regional State, local, and other agencies, both public and private, and individuals;

(2) to pay to witnesses whose depositions are taken or who are summoned before the Commission or any of its agents the same witness and mileage fees as are paid to witnesses in the courts of the United States;

(3) to furnish to persons subject to this title such technical assistance as they may request to further their compliance with this title or an order issued thereunder;

(4) upon the request of (i) any employer, whose employees or some of them, or (ii) any labor organization, whose members or some of them, refuse or threaten to refuse to cooperate in effectuating the provisions of this title, to assist in such effectuation by conciliation or such other remedial action as is provided by this title;

(5) to make such technical studies as are appropriate to effectuate the purposes and policies of this title and to make the results of such studies available to the public;

(6) to intervene in a civil action brought under section 706 by an aggrieved party against a respondent other than a government, governmental agency, or political subdivision.

(h) The Commission shall, in any of its educational or promotional activities, cooperate with other departments and agencies in the performance of such educational and promotional activities.

(i) All officers, agents, attorneys, and employees of the Commission shall be subject to the provisions of section 9 of the Act of August 2, 1939, as amended (the Hatch Act), notwithstanding any exemption contained in such section.

Prevention of Unlawful Employment Practices

SEC. 706. (a) The Commission is empowered, as hereinafter provided, to prevent any person from engaging in any unlawful employment practice as set forth in section 703 or 704 of this title.

(b) Whenever a charge is filed by or on behalf of a person claiming to be aggrieved, or by a member of the Commission, alleging that an employer, employment agency, labor organization, or joint labor-management committee controlling apprenticeship or other training or retraining, including on-the-job training programs, has engaged in an unlawful employment practice, the Commission shall serve a notice of the charge (including the date, place and circumstances of the alleged unlawful employment practice) on such employer, employment agency, labor organization, or joint labor-management com-

mittee (hereinafter referred to as the "respondent") within ten days, and shall make an investigation thereof. Charges shall be in writing under oath or affirmation and shall contain such information and be in such form as the Commission requires. Charges shall not be made public by the Commission. If the Commission determines after such investigation that there is not reasonable cause to believe that the charge is true, it shall dismiss the charge and promptly notify the person claiming to be aggrieved and the respondent of its action. In determining whether reasonable cause exists, the Commission shall accord substantial weight to final findings and orders made by State or local authorities in proceedings commenced under State or local law pursuant to the requirements of subsections (c) and (d). If the Commission determines after such investigation that there is reasonable cause to believe that the charge is true, the Commission shall endeavor to eliminate any such alleged unlawful employment practice by informal methods of conference, conciliation, and persuasion. Nothing said or done during and as a part of such informal endeavors may be made public by the Commission, its officers or employees, or used as evidence in a subsequent proceeding without the written consent of the persons concerned. Any person who makes public information in violation of this subsection shall be fined not more than $1,000 or imprisoned for not more than one year, or both. The Commission shall make its determination on reasonable cause as promptly as possible and, so far as practicable, not later than one hundred and twenty days from the filing of the charge or, where applicable under subsection (c) or (d) from the date upon which the Commission is authorized to take action with respect to the charge.
(c) In the case of an alleged unlawful employment practice occurring in a State, or political subdivision of a State, which has a State or local law prohibiting the unlawful employment practice alleged and establishing or authorizing a State or local authority to grant or seek relief from such practice or to institute criminal proceedings with respect thereto upon receiving notice thereof, no charge may be filed under subsection (a) by the person aggrieved before the expiration of sixty days after proceedings have been commenced under the State or local law, unless such proceedings have been earlier terminated, provided that such sixty-day period shall be extended to one hundred and twenty days during the first year after the effective date of such State or local law. If any requirement for the commencement of such proceedings is imposed by a State or local authority other than a requirement of the filing of a written and signed statement of the

facts upon which the proceeding is based, the proceeding shall be deemed to have been commenced for the purposes of this subsection at the time such statement is sent by registered mail to the appropriate State or local authority.

(d) In the case of any charge filed by a member of the Commission alleging an unlawful employment practice occurring in a State or political subdivision of a State which has a State or local law prohibiting the practice alleged and establishing or authorizing a State or local authority to grant or seek relief from such practice or to institute criminal proceedings with respect thereto upon receiving notice thereof, the Commission shall, before taking any action with respect to such charge, notify the appropriate State or local officials and, upon request, afford them a reasonable time, but not less than sixty days (provided that such sixty-day period shall be extended to one hundred and twenty days during the first year after the effective date of such State or local law), unless a shorter period is requested, to act under each State or local law to remedy the practice alleged.

(e) A charge under this section shall be filed within one hundred and eighty days after the alleged unlawful employment practice occurred and notice of the charge (including the date, place and circumstances of the alleged unlawful employment practice) shall be served upon the person against whom such charge is made within ten days thereafter, except that in a case of an unlawful employment practice with respect to which the person aggrieved has initially instituted proceedings with a State or local agency with authority to grant or seek relief from such practice or to institute criminal proceedings with respect thereto upon receiving notice thereof, such charge shall be filed by or on behalf of the person aggrieved within three hundred days after the alleged unlawful employment practice occurred, or within thirty days after receiving notice that the State or local agency has terminated the proceedings under the State or local law, whichever is earlier, and a copy of such charge shall be filed by the Commission with the State or local agency.

(f) (1) If within thirty days after a charge is filed with the Commission or within the thirty days after expiration of any period of reference under subsection (c) or (d), the Commission has been unable to secure from the respondent a conciliation agreement acceptable to the Commission, the Commission may bring a civil action against any respondent not a government, governmental agency, or political subdivision named in the charge. In the case of a respondent which is a government, governmental agency, or political subdivision, if the Commission has been unable to secure from the respondent a conciliation agreement acceptable to the Commission, the Commission shall take no further action and shall refer the case to the Attorney General who may bring a civil action against such respondent in the appropriate United States district court. The person or persons aggrieved shall have the right to intervene in a civil action brought by the Commission or the Attorney General in a case involving a government, governmental agency, or political subdivision. If a charge filed with the Commission pursuant to subsection (b) is dismissed by the Commission, or if within one hundred and eighty days from the filing of such charge or the expiration of any period of reference under subsection (c) or (d), whichever is later, the Commission has not filed a civil action under this section or the Attorney General has notified a civil action in a case involving a government, governmental agency, or political subdivision, or the Commission has not entered into a conciliation agreement to which the person aggrieved is a party, the Commission, or the Attorney General in a case involving a government, governmental agency, or political subdivision, shall so notify the person aggrieved within ninety days after the giving of such notice a civil action may be brought against the respondent named in the charge (A) by the person claiming to be aggrieved, or (B) if such charge was filed by a member of the Commission, by any person whom the charge alleges was aggrieved by the alleged unlawful employment practice. Upon application by the complainant and in such circumstances as the court may deem just, the court may appoint an attorney for such complainant and may authorize the commencement of the action without the payment of fees, costs, or security. Upon timely application, the court may, in its discretion, permit the Commission, or the Attorney General in a case involving a government, governmental agency, or political subdivision, to intervene in such civil action upon certification that the case is of general public importance. Upon request, the court may, in its discretion, stay further proceedings for not more than sixty days pending the termination of State or local proceedings described in subsections (c) or (d) of this section or further efforts of the Commission to obtain voluntary compliance.

(2) Whenever a charge is filed with the Commission and the Commission concludes on the basis of a preliminary investigation that prompt judicial action is necessary to carry out the purposes of this Act, the Commission, or the Attorney General in a case involving a government, govern-

mental agency, or political subdivision, may bring an action for appropriate temporary or preliminary relief pending final disposition of such charge. Any temporary restraining order or other order granting preliminary or temporary relief shall be issued in accordance with rule 65 of the Federal Rules of Civil Procedure. It shall be the duty of a court having jurisdiction over proceedings under this section to assign cases for hearing at the earliest practicable date and to cause such cases to be in every way expedited.

(3) Each United States district court and each United States court of a place subject to the jurisdiction of the United States shall have jurisdiction of actions brought under this title. Such an action may be brought in any judicial district in the State in which the unlawful employment practice is alleged to have been committed, in the judicial district in which the employment records relevant to such practice are maintained and administered, or in the judicial district in which the aggrieved person would have worked but for the alleged unlawful employment practice, but if the respondent is not found within any such district, such an action may be brought within the judicial district in which the respondent has his principal office. For purposes of sections 1404 and 1406 of title 28 of the United States Code, the judicial district in which the respondent has his principal office shall in all cases be considered a district in which the action might have been brought.

(4) It shall be the duty of the chief judge of the district (or in his absence, the acting chief judge) in which the case is pending immediately to designate a judge in such district to hear and determine the case. In the event that no judge in the district is available to hear and determine the case, the chief judge of the district, or the acting chief judge, as the case may be, shall certify this fact to the chief judge of the circuit (or in his absence, the acting chief judge) who shall then designate a district or circuit judge of the circuit to hear and determine the case.

(5) It shall be the duty of the judge designated pursuant to this subsection to assign the case for hearing at the earliest practicable date and to cause the case to be in every way expedited. If such judge has not scheduled the case for trial within one hundred and twenty days after issue has been joined, that judge may appoint a master pursuant to rule 53 of the Federal Rules of Civil Procedure.

(g) If the court finds that the respondent has intentionally engaged in or is intentionally engaging in an unlawful employment practice charged in the complaint, the court may enjoin the respondent from engaging in such unlawful employment practice, and order such affirmative action as may be appropriate, which may include, but is not limited to, reinstatement or hiring of employees, with or without back pay (payable by the employer, employment agency, or labor organization, as the case may be, responsible for the unlawful employment practice), or any other equitable relief as the court deems appropriate. Back pay liability shall not accrue from a date more than two years prior to the filing of a charge with the Commission. Interim earnings or amounts earnable with reasonable diligence by the person or persons discriminated against shall operate to reduce the back pay otherwise allowable. No order of the court shall require the admission or reinstatement of an individual as a member of a union, or the hiring, reinstatement, or promotion of an individual as an employee, or the payment to him of any back pay, if such individual was refused admission, suspended, or expelled, or was refused employment or advancement or was suspended or discharged for any reason other than discrimination on account of race, color, religion, sex, or national origin or in violation of section 704(a).

(h) The provisions of the Act entitled "An Act to amend the Judicial Code and to define and limit the jurisdiction of courts sitting in equity, and for other purposes," approved March 23, 1932 (29 U.S.C. 101–115), shall not apply with respect to civil actions brought under this section.

(i) In any case in which an employer, employment agency, or labor organization fails to comply with an order of a court issued in a civil action brought under this section, the Commission may commence proceedings to compel compliance with such order.

(j) Any civil action brought under this section and any proceedings brought under subsection (i) shall be subject to appeal as provided in sections 1291 and 1292, title 28, United States Code.

(k) In any action or proceeding under this title the court, in its discretion, may allow the prevailing party, other than the Commission or the United States, a reasonable attorney's fee as part of the costs, and the Commission and the United States shall be liable for costs the same as a private person.

SEC. 707. (a) Whenever the Attorney General has reasonable cause to believe that any person or group of persons is engaged in a pattern or practice of resistance to the full enjoyment of any of the rights secured by this title, and that the pattern or practice is of such a nature and is intended to deny the full exercise of the rights herein described, the Attorney General may bring a civil action in the appropriate district court of the United States by filing with it a complaint (1) signed by him (or in his absence the Acting Attorney General), (2) setting forth facts pertaining to such pattern or practice, and (3) requesting such relief, including an application for a permanent or temporary injunction, restraining order or other order against the person or persons responsible for such pattern or practice, as he deems necessary to insure the full enjoyment of the rights herein described.

(b) The district courts of the United States shall have and shall exercise jurisdiction of proceedings instituted pursuant to this section, and in any such proceeding the Attorney General may file with the clerk of such court a request that a court of three judges be convened to hear and determine the case. Such request by the Attorney General shall be accompanied by a certificate that, in his opinion, the case is of general public importance. A copy of the certificate and request for a three-judge court shall be immediately furnished by such clerk to the chief judge of the circuit (or in his absence, the presiding circuit judge of the circuit) in which the case is pending. Upon receipt of such request it shall be the duty of the chief judge of the circuit or the presiding circuit judge, as the case may be, to designate immediately three judges in such circuit, of whom at least one shall be a circuit judge and another of whom shall be a district judge of the court in which the proceeding was instituted, to hear and determine such case, and it shall be the duty of the judges so designated to assign the case for hearing at the earliest practicable date, to participate in the hearing and determination thereof, and to cause the case to be in every way expedited. An appeal from the final judgment of such court will lie to the Supreme Court.

In the event the Attorney General fails to file such a request in any such proceeding, it shall be the duty of the chief judge of the district (or in his absence, the acting chief judge) in which the case is pending immediately to designate a judge in such district to hear and determine the case. In the event that no judge in the district is available to hear and determine the case, the chief judge of the district, or the acting chief judge, as the case may be, shall certify this fact to the chief judge of the circuit (or in his absence, the acting chief judge) who shall then designate a district or circuit judge of the circuit to hear and determine the case.

It shall be the duty of the judge designated pursuant to this section to assign the case for hearing at the earliest practicable date and to cause the case to be in every way expedited.

(c) Effective two years after the date of enactment of the Equal Employment Opportunity Act of 1972, the functions of the Attorney General under this section shall be transferred to the Commission, together with such personnel, property, records, and unexpended balances of appropriations, allocations, and other funds employed, used, held, available, or to be made available in connection with such functions unless the President submits, and neither House of Congress vetoes, a reorganization plan pursuant to chapter 9, of title 5, United States Code, inconsistent with the provisions of this subsection. The Commission shall carry out such functions in accordance with subsections (d) and (e) of this section.

(d) Upon the transfer of functions provided for in subsection (c) of this section, in all suits commenced pursuant to this section prior to the date of such transfer, proceedings shall continue without abatement, all court orders and decrees shall remain in effect, and the Commission shall be substituted as a party for the United States of America, the Attorney General, or the Acting Attorney General, as appropriate.

(e) Subsequent to the date of enactment of the Equal Employment Opportunity Act of 1972, the Commission shall have authority to investigate and act on a charge of a pattern or practice of discrimination, whether filed by or on behalf of a person claiming to be aggrieved or by a member of the Commission. All such actions shall be conducted in accordance with the procedures set forth in section 706 of this Act.

Effect on State Laws

SEC. 708. Nothing in this title shall be deemed to exempt or relieve any person from any liability, duty, penalty, or punishment provided by any present or future law of any State or political subdivision of a State, other than any such law which purports to require or permit the doing of any act which would be an unlawful employment practice under this title.

Investigations, Inspections, Records, State Agencies

SEC. 709. (a) In connection with any investigation of a charge filed under section 706, the Commission or its designated representative shall at all reasonable times have access to, for the purposes of examination, and the right to copy any evidence of any person being investigated or proceeded against that relates to unlawful employment practices covered by this title and is relevant to the charge under investigation.

(b) The Commission may cooperate with State and local agencies charged with the administration of State fair employment practices laws and, with the consent of such agencies, may, for the purpose of carrying out its functions and duties under this title and within the limitation of funds appropriated specifically for such purpose, engage in and contribute to the cost of research and other projects of mutual interest undertaken by such agencies, and utilize the services of such agencies and their employees, and, notwithstanding any other provision of law, pay by advance or reimbursement such agencies and their employees for services rendered to assist the Commission in carrying out this title. In furtherance of such cooperative efforts, the Commission may enter into written agreements with such State or local agencies and such agreements may include provisions under which the Commission shall refrain from processing a charge in any cases or class of cases specified in such agreements or under which the Commission shall relieve any person or class of persons in such State or locality from requirements imposed under this section. The Commission shall rescind any such agreement whenever it determines that the agreement no longer serves the interest of effective enforcement of this title.

(c) Every employer, employment agency, and labor organization subject to this title shall (1) make and keep such records relevant to the determinations of whether unlawful employment practices have been or are being committed, (2) preserve such records for such periods, and (3) make such reports therefrom, as the Commission shall prescribe by regulation or order, after public hearing, as reasonable, necessary, or appropriate for the enforcement of this title or the regulations or orders thereunder. The Commission shall, by regulations, require each employer, labor organization, and joint labor-management committee subject to this title which controls an apprenticeship or other training program to maintain such records as are reasonably necessary to carry out the purpose of this title, including, but not limited to, a list of applicants who wish to participate in such program, including the chronological order in which applications were received, and to furnish to the Commission upon request, a detailed description of the manner in which persons are selected to participate in the apprenticeship or other training program. Any employer, employment agency, labor organization, or joint labor-management committee which believes that the application to it of any regulation or order issued under this section would result in undue hardship may apply to the Commission for an exemption from the application of such regulation or order, and, if such application for an exemption is denied, bring a civil action in the United States district court for the district where such records are kept. If the Commission or the court, as the case may be, finds that the application of the regulation or order to the employer, employment agency, or labor organization in question would impose an undue hardship, the Commission or the court, as the case may be, may grant appropriate relief. If any person required to comply with the provisions of this subsection fails or refuses to do so, the United States district court for the district in which such person is found, resides, or transacts business, shall, upon application of the Commission, or the Attorney General in a case involving a government, governmental agency or political subdivision, have jurisdiction to issue to such person an order requiring him to comply.

(d) In prescribing requirements pursuant to subsection (c) of this section, the Commission shall consult with other interested State and Federal agencies and shall endeavor to coordinate its requirements with those adopted by such agencies. The Commission shall furnish upon request and without cost to any State or local agency, charged with the administration of a fair employment practice law information obtained pursuant to subsection (c) of this section from any employer, employment agency, labor organization, or joint labor-management committee subject to the jurisdiction of such agency. Such information shall be furnished on the condition that it not be made public by the recipient agency prior to the institution of a proceeding under State or local law involving such information. If this condition is violated by a recipient agency, the Commission may decline to honor subsequent requests pursuant to this subsection.

(e) It shall be unlawful for any officer or employee of the Commission to make public in any manner whatever any information obtained by the Commission pursuant to its authority under this section prior to the institution of any proceeding under this title involving such information. Any officer or employee of the Commission who shall make public in any manner whatever any information in violation of this subsection shall be guilty of a misdemeanor and upon conviction thereof, shall be fined not more than $1,000, or imprisoned not more than one year.

Investigatory Powers

SEC. 710. For the purpose of all hearings and investigations conducted by the Commission or its duly authorized agents

or agencies, section 11 of the National Labor Relations
Act (49 Stat. 455; 29 U.S.C. 161) shall apply.

Notices to be Posted

SEC. 711. (a) Every employer, employment agency, and
labor organization, as the case may be, shall post and keep
posted in conspicuous places upon its premises where notices
to employees, applicants for employment, and members
are customarily posted a notice to be prepared or approved
by the Commission setting forth excerpts from, or summaries
of, the pertinent provisions of this title and information
pertinent to the filing of a complaint.

(b) A willful violation of this section shall be punishable
by a fine of not more than $100 for each separate offense.

Veterans' Preference

SEC. 712. Nothing contained in this title shall be construed
to repeal or modify any Federal, State, territorial, or local
law creating special rights or preference for veterans.

Rules and Regulations

SEC. 713. (a) The Commission shall have authority from time
to time to issue, amend, or rescind suitable procedural regulations to carry out the provisions of this title. Regulations issued
under the section shall be in conformity with the standards
and limitations of the Administrative Procedure Act.

(b) In any action or proceeding based on any alleged unlawful
employment practice, no person shall be subject to any liability or punishment for or on account of (1) the commission
by such person of an unlawful employment practice if he
pleads and proves that the act or omission complained of
was in good faith, in conformity with, and in reliance on
any written interpretation or opinion of the Commission,
or (2) the failure of such person to publish and file any information required by any provision of this title if he pleads
and proves that he failed to publish and file such information
in good faith, in conformity with the instructions of the
Commission issued under this title regarding the filing of
such information. Such a defense, if established, shall be
a bar to the action or proceeding, notwithstanding that (A)
after such act or omission, such interpretation or opinion
is modified or rescinded or is determined by judicial authority
to be invalid or of no legal effect, or (B) after publishing
or filing the description and annual reports, such publication
or filing is determined by judicial authority not to be in
conformity with the requirements of this title.

Forcibly Resisting the Commission or its Representatives

SEC. 714. The provisions of sections 111 and 1114 title 18, United States Code, shall apply to officers, agents, and employees of the Commission in the performance of their official duties. Notwithstanding the provisions of sections 111 and 1114 of title 18, United States Code, whoever in violation of the provisions of section 1114 of such title kills a person while engaged in or on account of the performance of his official functions under this Act shall be punished by imprisonment for any term of years or for life.

Transfer of Authority

Administration of the duties of the Equal Employment Opportunity Coordinating Council was transferred to the Equal Employment Opportunity Commission effective July 1, 1978, under the President's Reorganization Plan No. 1 of 1978.

Equal Employment Opportunity Coordinating Council

SEC. 715. There shall be established an Equal Employment Opportunity Coordinating Council (herein after referred to in this section as the Council) composed of the Secretary of Labor, the Chairman of the Equal Employment Opportunity Commission, the Attorney General, the Chairman of the United States Civil Service Commission, and the Chairman of the United States Civil Rights Commission, or their respective delegates. The Council shall have the responsibility for developing and implementing agreements, policies and practices designed to maximize effort, promote efficiency, and eliminate conflict, competition, duplication and inconsistency among the operations, functions and jurisdictions of the various departments, agencies and branches of the Federal government responsible for the implementation and enforcement of equal employment opportunity legislation, orders, and policies. On or before July 1 of each year, the Council shall transmit to the President and to the Congress a report of its activities, together with such recommendations for legislative or administrative changes as it concludes are desirable to further promote the purposes of this section.

Effective Date

SEC. 716. (a) This title shall become effective one year after the date of its enactment.
(b) Notwithstanding subsection (a), sections of this title

other than sections 703, 704, 706, and 707 shall become
effective immediately.

(c) The President shall, as soon as feasible after the enactment
of this title, convene one or more conferences for the purpose
of enabling the leaders of groups whose members will be
affected by this title to become familiar with the rights
afforded and obligations imposed by its provisions, and for
the purpose of making plans which will result in the fair
and effective administration of this title when all of its
provisions become effective. The President shall invite the
participation in such conference or conferences of (1) the
members of the President's Committee on Equal Employment
Opportunity, (2) the members of the Commission on Civil
Rights, (3) representatives of State and local agencies engaged
in furthering equal employment opportunity, (4) representatives of private agencies engaged in furthering equal employment opportunity, and (5) representatives of employers,
labor organizations, and employment agencies who will be
subject to this title.

Transfer of Authority

Enforcement of Section 717 was transferred to the Equal
Employment Opportunity Commission from the Civil Service
Commission (Office of Personnel Management) effective
January 1, 1979 under the President's Reorganization Plan
No. 1 of 1978.

Nondiscrimination in Federal Government Employment

SEC. 717. (a) All personnel actions affecting employees
or applicants for employment (except with regard to aliens
employed outside the limits of the United States) in military
departments as defined in section 102 of title 5, United
States Code, in executive agencies (other than the General
Accounting Office) as defined in section 105 of title 5, United
States Code (including employees and applicants for employment who are paid from nonappropriated funds), in the United
States Postal Service and the Postal Rate Commission, in
those units of the Government of the District of Columbia
having positions in the competitive service, and in those
units of the legislative and judicial branches of the Federal
Government having positions in the competitive service,
and in the Library of Congress shall be made free from any
discrimination based on race, color, religion, sex, or national
origin.

(b) Except as otherwise provided in this subsection, the Civil

Service Commission shall have authority to enforce the provisions of subsection (a) through appropriate remedies, including reinstatement or hiring of employees with or without back pay, as will effectuate the policies of this section, and shall issue such rules, regulations, orders, and instructions as it deems necessary and appropriate to carry out its responsibilities under this section. The Civil Service Commission shall—

(1) be responsible for the annual review and approval of a national and regional equal employment opportunity plan which each department and agency and each appropriate unit referred to in subsection (a) of this section shall submit in order to maintain an affirmative program of equal employment opportunity for all such employees and applicants for employment;

(2) be responsible for the review and evaluation of the operation of all agency equal employment opportunity programs, periodically obtaining and publishing (on at least a semiannual basis) progress reports from each such department, agency, or unit; and

(3) consult with and solicit the recommendations of interested individuals, groups, and organizations relating to equal employment opportunity.

The head of each such department, agency, or unit shall comply with such rules, regulations, orders, and instructions which shall include a provision that an employee or applicant for employment shall be notified of any final action taken on any complaint of discrimination filed by him thereunder. The plan submitted by each department, agency, and unit shall include, but not be limited to—

(1) provision for the establishment of training and education programs designed to provide a maximum opportunity for employees to advance so as to perform at their highest potential; and

(2) a description of the qualifications in terms of training and experience relating to equal employment opportunity for the principal and operating officials of each such department, agency, or unit responsible for carrying out the equal employment opportunity program and of the allocation of personnel and resources proposed by such department, agency, or unit to carry out its equal employment opportunity program. With respect to employment in the Library of Congress, authorities granted in this subsection to the Civil Service Commission shall be exercised by the Librarian of Congress.

(c) Within thirty days of receipt of notice of final action taken by a department, agency, or unit referred to in subsection 717(a), or by the Civil Service Commission upon an appeal from a decision or order of such department, agency, or unit on a complaint of discrimination based on race, color, religion, sex, or national origin, brought pursuant to subsection (a) of this section, Executive Order 11478 or any succeeding Executive orders, or after one hundred and eighty days from the filing of the initial charge with the department, agency, or unit or with the Civil Service Commission on appeal from a decision or order of such department, agency, or unit until such time as final action may be taken by a department, agency, or unit, an employee or applicant for employment, if aggrieved by the final disposition of his complaint, or by the failure to take final action on his complaint, may file a civil action as provided in section 706, in which civil action the head of the department, agency, or unit, as appropriate, shall be the defendant.

(d) The provisions of section 706(f) through (k), as applicable, shall govern civil actions brought hereunder.

(e) Nothing contained in this Act shall relieve any Government agency or official of its or his primary responsibility to assure nondiscrimination in employment as required by the Constitution and statutes or of its or his responsibilities under Executive Order 11478 relating to equal employment opportunity in the Federal Government.

Special Provisions with Respect to Denial, Termination, and Suspension of Government Contracts

SEC. 718. No Government contract, or portion thereof, with any employer, shall be denied, withheld, terminated, or suspended, by any agency or officer of the United States under any equal employment opportunity law or order, where such employer has an affirmative action plan which has previously been accepted by the Government for the same facility within the past twelve months without first according such employer full hearing and adjudication under the provisions of title 5, United States Code, section 554, and the following pertinent sections: Provided, That if such employer has deviated substantially from such previously agreed to affirmative action plan, this section shall not apply: Provided further, That for the purposes of this section an affirmative action plan shall be deemed to have been accepted by the Government at the time the appropriate compliance agency has accepted such plan unless within forty-five days thereafter the Office of Federal Contract Compliance has disapproved such plan.

Appendix B
The Age Discrimination in Employment Act of 1967, as Amended

An Act

To prohibit age discrimination in employment

Be it enacted by the Senate and House of Representatives of the United States of America in Congress assembled, that this Act may be cited as the "Age Discrimination in Employment Act of 1967".

Statement of Findings and Purpose

SEC. 2. (a) The Congress hereby finds and declares that—

(1) in the face of rising productivity and affluence, older workers find themselves disadvantaged in their efforts to retain employment, and especially to regain employment when displaced from jobs;

(2) the setting of arbitrary age limits regardless of potential for job performance has become a common practice, and certain otherwise desirable practices may work to the disadvantage of older persons;

(3) the incidence of unemployment, especially longterm unemployment with resultant deterioration of skill, morale, and employer acceptability is, relative to the younger ages, high among older workers; their numbers are great and growing; and their employment problems grave;

(4) the existence in industries affecting commerce, of arbitrary discrimination in employment because of age, burdens commerce and the free flow of goods in commerce.

(b) It is therefore the purpose of this Act to promote employment of older persons based on their ability rather than age; to prohibit arbitrary age discrimination in the employment; to help employers and workers find ways of meeting problems arising from the impact of age on employment.

Education and Research Program

SEC. 3. (a) The Secretary of Labor shall undertake studies and provide information to labor unions, management, and the general public concerning the needs and abilities of older workers, and their potentials for continued employment and contribution to the economy. In order to achieve the purposes of this Act, the Secretary of Labor shall carry on a continuing program of education and information, under which he may, among other measures—

(1) undertake research, and promote research, with a view to reducing barriers to the employment of older persons, and the promotion of measures for utilizing their skills;

(2) publish and otherwise make available to employers, professional societies, the various media of communication, and other interested persons the findings of studies and other materials for the promotion of employment;

(3) foster through the public employment service system and through cooperative effort the development of facilities of public and private agencies for expanding the opportunities and potentials of older persons;

(4) sponsor and assist State and community informational and educational programs.

(b) Not later than six months after the effective date of this Act, the Secretary shall recommend to the Congress any measures he may deem desirable to change the lower or upper age limits set forth in section 12.

Prohibition of Age Discrimination

SEC. 4. (a) It shall be unlawful for an employer—

(1) to fail or refuse to hire or to discharge any individual or otherwise discriminate against any individual with respect to his compensation, terms, conditions, or privileges of employment, because of such individual's age;

(2) to limit, segregate, or classify his employees in any way which would deprive or tend to deprive any individual of employment opportunities or otherwise adversely affect his status as an employee, because of such individual's age; or

(3) to reduce the wage rate of any employee in order to comply with this Act.

(b) It shall be unlawful for an employment agency to fail

or refuse to refer for employment, or otherwise to discriminate against, any individual because of such individual's age, or to classify or refer for employment any individual on the basis of such individual's age.

(c) It shall be unlawful for a labor organization—

(1) to exclude or to expel from its membership, or otherwise to discriminate against, any individual because of his age;

(2) to limit, segregate, or classify its membership, or to classify or fail or refuse to refer for employment any individual, in any way which would deprive or tend to deprive any individual of employment opportunities, or would limit such employment opportunities or otherwise adversely affect his status as an employee or as an applicant for employment, because of such individual's age;

(3) to cause or attempt to cause an employee to discriminate against an individual in violation of this section.

(d) It shall be unlawful for an employer to discriminate against any of his employees or applicants for employment, for an employment agency to discriminate against any individual, or for a labor organization to discriminate against any member thereof or applicant for membership, because such individual, member or applicant for membership has opposed any practice made unlawful by this section, or because such individual, member or applicant for membership has made a charge, testified, assisted, or participated in any manner in an investigation, proceeding, or litigation under this Act.

(e) It shall be unlawful for an employer, labor organization, or employment agency to print or publish, or cause to be printed or published, any notice or advertisement relating to employment by such an employer or membership in or any classification or referral for employment by such a labor organization, or relating to any classification or referral for employment by such an employment agency, indicating any preference, limitation, specification, or discrimination, based on age.

(f) It shall not be unlawful for an employer, employment agency, or labor organization—

(1) to take any action otherwise prohibited under subsections (a), (b), (c), or (e) of this section where age is a bona fide occupational qualification reasonably necessary to the normal operation of the particular business, or where the differentiation is based on reasonable factors other than age, or where such practices involve an employee in a workplace in a foreign country, and compliance with such subsections would cause such employer, or a corporation controlled by such employer, to violate the laws of the country in which such workplace is located;

(2) to observe the terms of a bona fide seniority system or any bona fide employee benefit plan such as a retirement, pension, or insurance plan, which is not a subterfuge to evade the purposes of this Act, except that no such employee benefit plan shall excuse the failure to hire any individual, and no such seniority system or employee benefit plan shall require or permit the involuntary retirement of any individual specified by section 12(a) of this Act because of the age of such individual; or

(3) to discharge or otherwise discipline an individual for good cause.

(g) (1) For purposes of this section, any employer must provide that any employee aged 65 or older, and any employee's spouse aged 65 or older, shall be entitled to coverage under any group health plan offered to such employees under the same conditions as any employee, and the spouse of such employee, under age 65.

(2) For purposes of paragraph (1), the term "group health plan" has the meaning given to such term in section 162(i)(2) of the Internal Revenue Code of 1954 [96 Stat. 353, 29 U.S.C. § 623(g), as amended July 18, 1984, P.L. 98-369, 98 Stat. 1063, effective January 1, 1985, and further amended May 1, 1986, P.L. 99-272, Section 9201(b), 100 Stat. 171, to change the age range of affected employees and employee spouses from "65 through 69" to "65 or older".]

(h) (1) If an employer controls a corporation whose place of incorporation is in a foreign country, any practice by such corporation prohibited under this section shall be presumed to be such practice by such employer.

(2) The prohibitions of this section shall not apply where the employer is a foreign person not controlled by an American employer.

(3) For the purpose of this subsection the determination of whether an employer controls a corporation shall be based upon the—

(A) interrelation of operations,

(B) common management,

(C) centralized control of labor relations, and

(D) common ownership or financial control, of the employer and the corporation.

(i)[1] It shall not be unlawful for an employer which is a State, a political subdivision of a State, an agency or instrumentality of a State or a political subdivision of a State, or an interstate agency to fail or refuse to hire or to discharge any individual

----

[1]Automatically repealed December 31, 1993.

(1) with respect to the employment of an individual as a firefighter or as a law enforcement officer and the individual has attained the age of hiring or retirement in effect under applicable State or local law on March 3, 1983, and

(2) pursuant to a bona fide hiring or retirement plan that is not a subterfuge to evade the purposes of this Act.

(i) (1)^2 Except as otherwise provided in this subsection, it shall be unlawful for an employer, an employment agency, a labor organization, or any combination thereof to establish or maintain an employee pension benefit plan which requires or permits—

(A) in the case of a defined benefit plan, the cessation of an employee's benefit accrual, or the reduction of the rate of an employee's benefit accrual, because of age, or

(B) in the case of a defined contribution plan, the cessation of allocations to an employee's account, or the reduction of the rate at which amounts are allocated to an employee's account, because of age.

(2) Nothing in this section shall be construed to prohibit an employer, employment agency, or labor organization from observing any provision of an employee pension benefit plan to the extent that such provision imposes (without regard to age) a limitation on the amount of benefits that the plan provides or a limitation on the number of years of service or years of participation which are taken into account for purposes of determining benefit accrual under the plan.

(3) In the case of any employee who, as of the end of any plan year under a defined benefit plan, has attained normal retirement age under such plan—

(A) if distribution of benefits under such plan with respect to such employee has commenced as of the end of such plan year, then any requirement of this subsection for continued accrual of benefits under such plan with respect to such employee during such plan year shall be treated as satisfied to the extent of the actuarial equivalent of in-service distribution of benefits, and

(B) if distribution of benefits under such plan with respect to such employee has not commenced as of the end of such year in accordance with section 206(a)(3) of the Employee Retirement Income Security Act of 1974 and section 401(a)(14)(C) of the Internal Revenue Code of 1986, and the payment of benefits under such plan with respect to such employee is not suspended during such plan year pursuant

---

^{2}Due to a drafting error, Congress added this section as a second Section 4(i).

to section 203(a)(3)(B) of the Employee Retirement Income Security Act of 1974 or section 411(a)(3)(B) of the Internal Revenue Code of 1986, then any requirement of this subsection for continued accrual of benefits under such plan with respect to such employee during such plan year shall be treated as satisfied to the extent of any adjustment in the benefit payable under the plan during such plan year attributable to the delay in the distribution of benefits after the attainment of normal retirement age.

The provisions of this paragraph shall apply in accordance with regulations of the Secretary of the Treasury. Such regulations shall provide for the application of the preceding provisions of this paragraph to all employee pension benefit plans subject to this subsection and may provide for the application of such provisions, in the case of any such employee, with respect to any period of time within a plan year.

(4) Compliance with the requirements of this subsection with respect to an employee pension benefit plan shall constitute compliance with the requirements of this section relating to benefit accrual under such plan.

(5) Paragraph (1) shall not apply with respect to any employee who is a highly compensated employee (within the meaning of section 414(q) of the Internal Revenue Code of 1986) to the extent provided in regulations prescribed by the Secretary of the Treasury for purposes of precluding discrimination in favor of highly compensated employees within the meaning of subchapter D of chapter 1 of the Internal Revenue Code of 1986.

(6) A plan shall not be treated as failing to meet the requirements of paragraph (1) solely because the subsidized portion of any early retirement benefit is disregarded in determining benefit accruals.

(7) Any regulations prescribed by the Secretary of the Treasury pursuant of clause (v) of section 411(b)(1)(H) of the Internal Revenue Code of 1986 and subparagraphs (C) and (D) of section 411(b)(2) of such Code shall apply with respect to the requirements of this subsection in the same manner and to the same extent as such regulations apply with respect to the requirements of such sections 411(b)(1)(H) and 411(b)(2).

(8) A plan shall not be treated as failing to meet the requirements of this section solely because such plan provides a normal retirement age described in section 3(24)(B) of the Employee Retirement Income Security Act of 1974 and section 411(a)(8)(B) of the Internal Revenue Code of 1986.

(9) For purposes of this subsection—

(A) The terms "employee pension benefit plan," "defined benefit plan," "defined contribution plan," and "normal retirement age" have the meanings provided such terms in section 3 of the Employee Retirement Income Security Act of 1974 (29 U.S.C. 1002).

(B) The term "compensation" has the meaning provided by section 414(s) of the Internal Revenue Code of 1986.

Study by Secretary of Labor

SEC. 5 (a)(1) The Secretary of Labor is directed to undertake an appropriate study of institutional and other arrangements giving rise to involuntary retirement, and report his findings and any appropriate legislative recommendations to the President and to the Congress. Such study shall include—

(A) an examination of the effect of the amendment made by section 3(a) of the Age Discrimination in Employment Act Amendments of 1978 in raising the upper age limitation established by section 12(a) of this Act to 70 years of age;

(B) a determination of the feasibility of eliminating such limitations;

(C) a determination of the feasibility of raising such limitation above 70 years of age; and

(D) an examination of the effect of the exemption contained in section 12(c), relating to certain executive employees, and the exemption contained in section 12(d), relating to tenured teaching personnel.

(2) The Secretary may undertake the study required by paragraph (1) of this subsection directly or by contract or other arrangement.

(b) The report required by subsection (a) of this section shall be transmitted to the President and the Congress as an interim report not later than January 1, 1981, and in final form not later than January 1, 1982.

Transfer of Functions

All functions relating to age discrimination administration and enforcement vested by section 6 in the Secretary of Labor or the Civil Service Commission were transferred to the Equal Employment Opportunity Commission effective January 1, 1979 under the President's Reorganization Plan No. 1.

Administration

SEC. 6. The Secretary shall have the power—
(a) to make delegations, to appoint such agents and employees, and to pay for technical assistance on a fee for service basis, as he deems necessary to assist him in the performance of his functions under this Act;
(b) to cooperate with regional, State, local, and other agencies, and to cooperate with and furnish technical assistance to employers, labor organizations, and employment agencies to aid in effectuating the purposes of this Act.

Recordkeeping, Investigation, and Enforcement

SEC. 7. (a) The Equal Employment Opportunity Commission shall have the power to make investigations and require the keeping of records necessary or appropriate for the administration of this Act in accordance with the powers and procedures provided in sections 9 and 11 of the Fair Labor Standards Act of 1938, as amended (29 U.S.C. 209 and 211).
(b) The provisions of this Act shall be enforced in accordance with the powers, remedies, and procedures provided in sections 11(b), 16 (except for subsection (a) thereof), and 17 of the Fair Labor Standards Act of 1983, as amended (29 U.S.C. 211(b), 216, 217), and subsection (c) of this section. Any act prohibited under section 4 of this Act shall be deemed to be a prohibited act under section 15 of the Fair Labor Standards Act of 1938, as amended (29 U.S.C. 215). Amounts owing to a person as a result of a violation of this Act shall be deemed to be unpaid minimum wages or unpaid overtime compensation for purposes of sections 16 and 17 of the Fair Labor Standards Act of 1938, as amended (29 U.S.C. 216, 217): Provided, That liquidated damages shall be payable only in cases of willful violations of this Act. In any action brought to enforce this Act the court shall have jurisdiction to grant such legal or equitable relief as may be appropriate to effectuate the purposes of this Act, including without limitation judgments compelling employment, reinstatement or promotion, or enforcing the liability for amounts deemed to be unpaid minimum wages or unpaid overtime compensation under this section. Before instituting any action under this section, EEOC shall attempt to eliminate the discriminatory practice or practices alleged, and to effect voluntary compliance with requirements of this Act through informal methods of conciliation, conference, and persuasion.
(c)(1) Any person aggrieved may bring a civil action in any

court of competent jurisdiction for such legal or equitable relief as will effectuate the purposes of this Act: Provided, That the right of any person to bring such action shall terminate upon the commencement of an action by EEOC to enforce the right of such employee under this Act.

(2) In an action brought under paragraph (1), a person shall be entitled to a trial by jury of any issue of fact in any such action for recovery of amounts owing as a result of a violation of this Act, regardless of whether equitable relief is sought by any party in such action.

(d) No civil action may be commenced by an individual under this section until 60 days after a charge alleging unlawful discrimination has been filed with EEOC. Such a charge shall be filed—

(1) within 180 days after the alleged unlawful practice occurred; or

(2) in a case to which section 14(b) applies, within 300 days after the alleged unlawful practice occurred, or within 30 days after receipt by the individual of notice of termination of proceedings under State law, whichever is earlier.

Upon receiving such a charge, EEOC shall promptly notify all persons named in such charge as prospective defendants in the action and shall promptly seek to eliminate any alleged unlawful practice by informal methods of conciliation, conference, and persuasion.

(e)(1) Sections 6 and 10 of the Portal-to-Portal Act of 1947 shall apply to actions under this Act.

(2) For the period during which EEOC is attempting to effect voluntary compliance with requirements of this Act through informal methods of conciliation, conference, and persuasion pursuant to subsection (b), the statute of limitations as provided in section 6 of the Portal-to-Portal Act of 1947 shall be tolled, but in no event for a period in excess of one year.

Notice to be Posted

SEC. 8. Every employer, employment agency, and labor organization shall post and keep posted in conspicuous places upon its premises a notice to be prepared or approved by EEOC setting forth information as EEOC deems appropriate to effectuate the purposes of this Act.

Rules and Regulations

SEC. 9. In accordance with the provisions of subchapter

II of chapter 5 of title 5, United States Code, EEOC may
issue such rules and regulations as it may consider necessary
or appropriate for carrying out this Act, and may establish
such reasonable exemptions to and from any or all provisions
of this Act as it may find necessary and proper in the public
interest.

Criminal Penalties

SEC. 10. Whoever shall forcibly resist, oppose, impede, intimi-
date or interfere with a duly authorized representative of
EEOC while it is engaged in the performance of duties under
this Act shall be punished by a fine of not more than $500
or by imprisonment for not more than one year, or both:
Provided, however, That no person shall be imprisoned under
this section except when there has been a prior conviction
hereunder.

Definitions

SEC. 11. For the purposes of this Act—
(a) The term "person" means one or more individuals, partnerships, associations, labor organizations, corporations, business
trusts, legal representatives, or any organized groups of
persons.
(b) The term "employer" means a person engaged in an industry
affecting commerce who has twenty or more employees
for each working day in each of twenty or more calendar
weeks in the current or preceding calendar year: Provided,
That prior to June 30, 1968, employers having fewer than
fifty employees shall not be considered employers. The term
also means (1) any agent of such a person, and (2) a State
or political subdivision of a State and any agency or instrumentality of a State or a political subdivision of a State, and
any interstate agency, but such term does not include the
United States, or a corporation wholly owned by the Government of the United States.
(c) The term "employment agency" means any person regularly
undertaking with or without compensation to procure employees for an employer and includes an agent of such a
person; but shall not include an agency of the United States.
(d) The term "labor organization" means a labor organization
engaged in an industry affecting commerce, and any agent
of such an organization, and includes any organization of
any kind, any agency, or employee representation committee,
group, association, or plan so engaged in which employees
participate and which exists for the purpose, in whole or

in part, of dealing with employers concerning grievances, labor disputes, wages, rates of pay, hours, or other terms or conditions of employment, and any conference, general committee, joint or system board, or joint council so engaged which is subordinate to a national or international labor organization.

(e) A labor organization shall be deemed to be engaged in an industry affecting commerce if (1) it maintains or operates a hiring hall or hiring office which procures employees for an employer or procures for employees opportunities to work for an employer, or (2) the number of its members (or, where it is a labor organization composed of other labor organizations or their representatives, if the aggregate number of the members of such other labor organization) is fifty or more prior to July 1, 1968, or twenty-five or more on or after July 1, 1968, and such labor organization—

(1) is the certified representative of employees under the provisions of the National Labor Relations Act, as amended, or the Railway Labor Act, as amended; or

(2) although not certified, is a national or international labor organization or a local labor organization recognized or acting as the representative of employees of an employer or employers engaged in an industry affecting commerce; or

(3) has chartered a local labor organization or subsidiary body which is representing or actively seeking to represent employees of employers within the meaning of paragraph (1) or (2); or

(4) has been chartered by a labor organization representing or actively seeking to represent employees within the meaning of paragraph (1) or (2) as the local or subordinate body through which such employees may enjoy membership or become affiliated with such labor organization; or

(5) is a conference, general committee, joint or system board, or joint council subordinate to a national or international labor organization, which includes a labor organization engaged in an industry affecting commerce within the meaning of any of the preceding paragraphs of this subsection.

(f) The term "employee" means an individual employed by any employer except that the term "employee" shall not include any person elected to public office in any State or political subdivision of any State by the qualified voters thereof, or any person chosen by such officer to be on such officer's personal staff, or an appointee on the policymaking level or an immediate adviser with respect to the exercise of the constitutional or legal powers of the office. The exemption set forth in the preceding sentence shall not include

employees subject to the civil service laws of a State government, governmental agency, or political subdivision. The
term "employee" includes any individual who is a citizen
of the United States employed by an employer in a workplace
in a foreign country.

(g) The term "commerce" means trade, traffic, commerce,
transportation, transmission, or communication among the
several States; or between a State and any place outside
thereof; or within the District of Columbia, or a possession
of the United States; or between points in the same State
but through a point outside thereof.

(h) The term "industry affecting commerce" means any activity, business, or industry in commerce or in which a labor
dispute would hinder or obstruct commerce or the free flow
of commerce and includes any activity or industry "affecting
commerce" within the meaning of the Labor-Management
Reporting and Disclosure Act of 1959.

(i) The term "State" includes a State of the United States,
the District of Columbia, Puerto Rico, the Virgin Islands,
American Samoa, Guam, Wake Island, the Canal Zone, and
Outer Continental Shelf lands defined in the Outer Continental
Shelf Lands Act.

(j) The term "firefighter" means an employee, the duties
of whose position are primarily to perform work directly
connected with the control and extinguishment of fires or
the maintenance and use of firefighting apparatus and equipment, including an employee engaged in this activity who
is transferred to a supervisory or administrative position.

(k) The term "law enforcement officer" means an employee,
the duties of whose position are primarily the investigation,
apprehension, or detention of individuals suspected or con-
victed of offenses against the criminal laws of a State, including an employee engaged in this activity who is transferred
to a supervisory or administrative position. For the purpose
of this subsection, "detention" includes the duties of employees
assigned to guard individuals incarcerated in any penal
institution.

Age Limitation

SEC. 12. (a) The prohibitions in this Act (except the provisions
of section 4(g)) shall be limited to individuals who are at
least 40 years of age.

(b) In the case of any personnel action affecting employees
or applicants for employment which is subject to the provisions
of section 15 of this Act, the prohibitions established in
section 15 of this Act shall be limited to individuals who
are at least 40 years of age.

(c)(1) Nothing in this Act shall be construed to prohibit compulsory retirement of any employee who has attained 65 years of age, and who, for the 2-year period immediately before retirement, is employed in a bona fide executive or a high policymaking position, if such employee is entitled to an immediate nonforfeitable annual retirement benefit from a pension, profit-sharing, savings, or deferred compensation plan, or any combination of such plans, of the employer of such employee, which equals, in the aggregate, at least $44,000.

(2) In applying the retirement benefit test of paragraph (1) of this subsection, if any such retirement benefit is in a form other than a straight life annuity (with no ancillary benefits), or if employees contribute to any such plan or make rollover contributions, such benefit shall be adjusted in accordance with regulations prescribed by EEOC, after consultation with the Secretary of the Treasury, so that the benefit is the equivalent of a straight life annuity (with no ancillary benefits) under a plan to which employees do not contribute and under which no rollover contributions are made.

(d)[3] Nothing in this Act shall be construed to prohibit compulsory retirement of any employee who has attained 70 years of age, and who is serving under a contract of unlimited tenure (or similar arrangement providing for unlimited tenure) at an institution of higher education (as defined by section 1201(a) of the Higher Education Act of 1965).

Annual Report

SEC. 13. EEOC shall submit annually in January a report to the Congress covering its activities for the preceding year and including such information, data, and recommendations for futher legislation in connection with the matters covered by this Act as it may find advisable. Such report shall contain an evaluation and appraisal by EEOC of the effect of the minimum and maximum ages established by this Act, together with its recommendations to the Congress. In making such evaluation and appraisal, EEOC shall take into consideration any changes which may have occurred in the general age level of the population, the effect of the Act upon workers not covered by its provisions, and such other factors as it may deem pertinent.

---

[3] Automatically repealed December 31, 1993.

Federal-State Relationship

SEC. 14. (a) Nothing in this Act shall affect the jurisdiction
of any agency of any State performing like functions with
regard to discriminatory employment practices on account
of age except that upon commencement of action under
this Act such action shall supersede any State action.
(b) In the case of an alleged unlawful practice occurring
in a State which has a law prohibiting discrimination in employment because of age and establishing or authorizing
a State authority to grant or seek relief from such discriminatory practice, no suit may be brought under section 7 of
this Act before the expiration of sixty days after proceedings
have been commenced under the State law, unless such proceedings have been earlier terminated: Provided, That such
sixty-day period shall be extended to one hundred and twenty
days during the first year after the effective date of such
State law. If any requirement for the commencement of
such proceedings is imposed by a State authority other than
a requirement of the filing of a written and signed statement
of the facts upon which the proceeding is based, the proceeding shall be deemed to have been commenced for the purposes
of this subsection at the time such statement is sent by
registered mail to the appropriate State authority.

**Nondiscrimination on Account of Age in Federal Government
Employment**

SEC. 15. (a) All personnel actions affecting employees or
applicants for employment who are at least 40 years of
age (except personnel actions with regard to aliens employed
outside the limits of the United States) in military departments as defined in section 102 of title 5, United States
Code, in executive agencies as defined in section 105 of
title 5, United States Code (including employees and applicants
for employment who are paid from nonappropriated funds),
in the United States Postal Service and the Postal Rate
Commission, in those units in the government of the District
of Columbia having positions in the competitive service,
and in those units of the legislative and judicial branches
of the Federal Government having positions in the competitive
service, and in the Library of Congress shall be made free
from any discrimination based on age.
(b) Except as otherwise provided in this subsection, EEOC
is authorized to enforce the provisions of subsection (a) of
this section through appropriate remedies, including reinstatement or hiring of employees with or without backpay, as

will effectuate the policies of this section. EEOC shall issue such rules, regulations, orders and instructions as it deems necessary and appropriate to carry out its responsibilities under this section. EEOC shall—

(1) be responsible for the review and evaluation of the operation of all agency programs designed to carry out the policy of this section, periodically obtaining and publishing (on at least a semiannual basis) progress reports from each department, agency, or unit referred to in subsection (a) of this section;

(2) consult with and solicit the recommendations of interested individuals, groups, and organizations relating to nondiscrimination in employment on account of age; and

(3) provide for the acceptance and processing of complaints of discrimination in Federal employment on account of age.

The head of each such department, agency, or unit shall comply with such rules, regulations, orders, and instructions of EEOC which shall include a provision that an employee or applicant for employment shall be notified of any final action taken on any complaint of discrimination filed by him thereunder. Reasonable exemptions to the provisions of this section may be established by the Commission but only when the Commission has established a maximum age requirement on the basis of a determination that age is a bona fide occupational qualification necessary to the performance of the duties of the position. With respect to employment in the Library of Congress, authorities granted in this subsection to EEOC shall be exercised by the Librarian of Congress.

(c) Any person aggrieved may bring a civil action in any Federal district court of competent jurisdiction for such legal or equitable relief as will effectuate the purposes of this Act.

(d) When the individual has not filed a complaint concerning age discrimination with the Commission, no civil action may be commenced by an individual under this section until the individual has given the Commission not less than thirty days' notice of an intent to file such action. Such notice shall be filed within one hundred and eighty days after the alleged unlawful practice occurred. Upon receiving a notice of intent to sue, the Commission shall promptly notify all persons named therein as prospective defendants in the action and take any appropriate action to assure the elimination of any unlawful practice.

(e) Nothing contained in this section shall relieve any Government agency or official of the responsibility to assure non-discrimination on account of age in employment as required under any provision of Federal law.

(f) Any personnel action of any department, agency or other entity referred to in subsection (a) of this section shall not be subject to or affected by, any provision of this Act, other than the provisions of section 12(b) of this Act and the provisions of this section.

(g)(1) EEOC shall undertake a study relating to the effects of the amendments made to this section by the Age Discrimination in Employment Act Amendments of 1978, and the effects of section 12(b) of this Act, as added by the Age Discrimination in Employment Act Amendments of 1978.

(2) EEOC shall transmit a report to the President and to the Congress containing the findings of the Commission resulting from the study of the Commission under paragraph (1) of this subsection. Such report shall be transmitted no later than January 1, 1980.

Effective Date

SEC. 16. This Act shall become effective one hundred and eighty days after enactment, except (a) that the Secretary of Labor may extend the delay in effective date of any provision of this Act up to an additional ninety days thereafter if he finds that such time is necessary in permitting adjustments to the provisions hereof, and (b) that on or after the date of enactment the Secretary of Labor (EEOC) is authorized to issue such rules and regulations as may be necessary to carry out its provisions.

Appropriations

SEC. 17. There are hereby authorized to be appropriated such sums as may be necessary to carry out this Act.

Approved December 15, 1967.

Appendix C
The Equal Pay Act of 1963, The Fair Labor Standards Act of 1938, as Amended

The Equal Pay Act of 1963*

Minimum Wages

SEC. 6(d)(1) No employer having employees subject to any provisions of this section shall discriminate, within any establishment in which such employees are employed, between employees on the basis of sex by paying wages to employees in such establishment at a rate less than the rate at which he pays wages to employees of the opposite sex in such establishment for equal work on jobs the performance of which require equal skill, effort, and responsibility, and which are performed under similar working conditions, except where such payment is made pursuant to (i) a seniority system; (ii) a merit system; (iii) a system which measures earnings by quantity or quality of production; or (iv) a differential based on any other factor other than sex: Provided, That an employer who is paying a wage rate differential in violation of this subsection shall not, in order to comply with the provisions of this subsection, reduce the wage rate of any employee.

(2) No labor organization, or its agents, representing employees of an employer having employees subject to any provisions of this section shall cause or attempt to cause such an employer to discriminate against an employee in violation of paragraph (1) of this subsection.

---

*The Equal Pay Act of 1963 begins at this section of Fair Labor Standards Act of 1938.

(3) For purposes of administration and enforcement, any amounts owing to any employee which have been withheld in violation of this subsection shall be deemed to be unpaid minimum wages or unpaid overtime compensation under this Act.

(4) As used in this subsection, the term "labor organization" means any organization of any kind, or any agency or employee representation committee or plan, in which employees participate and which exists for the purpose, in whole or in part, of dealing with employers concerning grievances, labor disputes, wages, rates of pay, hours of employment, or conditions of work.

Additional Provisions of Equal Pay Act of 1963
(77 Stat. 56)
[Public Law 88-38]
[88th Congress, S. 1409]
[June 10, 1963]

An Act

To prohibit discrimination on account of sex in the payment of wages by employers engaged in commerce or in the production of goods for commerce.

Be it enacted by the Senate and House of Representatives of the United States of America in Congress assembled, That this Act may be cited as the "Equal Pay Act of 1963".

Declaration of Purpose

SEC. 2. (a) The Congress hereby finds that the existence in industries engaged in commerce or in the production of goods for commerce of wage differentials based on sex—

(1) depresses wages and living standards for employees necessary for their health and efficiency;

(2) prevents the maximum utilization of the available labor resources;

(3) tends to cause labor disputes, thereby burdening, affecting, and obstructing commerce;

(4) burdens commerce and the free flow of goods in commerce; and

(5) constitutes an unfair method of competition.

(b) It is hereby declared to be the policy of this Act, through exercise by Congress of its power to regulate commerce among the several States and with foreign nations, to correct the conditions above referred to in such industries.

[Section 3 of the Equal Pay Act of 1963 amends section

6 of the Fair Labor Standards Act by adding a new subsection (d). The amendment is incorporated in the revised text of the Fair Labor Standards Act.]

Effective Date

SEC. 4. The amendments made by this Act shall take effect upon the expiration of one year from the date of its enactment: Provided, That in the case of employees covered by a bona fide collective bargaining agreement in effect at least thirty days prior to the date of enactment of this Act, entered into by a labor organization (as defined in section 6(d)(4) of the Fair Labor Standards Act of 1938, as amended), the amendments made by this Act shall take effect upon the termination of such collective bargaining agreement or upon the expiration of two years from the date of enactment of this Act, whichever shall first occur.

Approved June 10, 1963, 12m.

In the following excerpts from the Fair Labor Standards Act of 1938, as amended, authority given to the Secretary of Labor is exercised by the Equal Employment Opportunity Commission for purposes of enforcing the Equal Pay Act of 1963.

Attendance of Witnesses

SEC. 9. For the purpose of any hearing or investigation provided for in this Act, the provisions of sections 9 and 10 (relating to the attendance of witnesses and the production of books, papers and documents) of the Federal Trade Commission Act of September 16, 1914, as amended (U.S.C., 1934 edition, title 15, secs. 49 and 50), are hereby made applicable to the jurisdiction, powers, and duties of the Secretary of Labor and the industry committees.

Investigations, Inspections, Records, and Homework Regulations

SEC. 11. (a) The Secretary of Labor or his designated representatives may investigate and gather data regarding the wages, hours, and other conditions and practices of employment in any industry subject to this Act, and may enter and inspect such places and such records (and make such transcriptions thereof), question such employees, and investigate such facts, conditions, practices, or matters as he may deem

necessary or appropriate to determine whether any person
has violated any provision of this Act, or which may aid
in the enforcement of the provisions of this Act. Except
as provided in section 12 and in subsection (b) of this section,
the Secretary shall utilize the bureaus and divisions of the
Department of Labor for all the investigations and inspections
necessary under this section. Except as provided in section
12, the Secretary shall bring all actions under section 17
to restrain violations of this Act.

(b) With the consent and cooperation of State agencies charged
with the administration of State labor laws, the Secretary
of Labor may, for the purposes of carrying out his functions
and duties under this Act, utilize the services of State and
local agencies and their employees and, notwithstanding
any other provision of law, may reimburse such State and
local agencies and their employees for services rendered
for such purposes.

(c) Every employer subject to any provision of this Act or
of any order issued under this Act shall make, keep, and
preserve such records of the persons employed by him and
of the wages, hours, and other conditions and practices of
employment maintained by him, and shall preserve such
records for such periods of time, and shall make such reports
therefrom to the Secretary as he shall prescribe by regulation
or order as necessary or appropriate for the enforcement
of the provisions of this Act or the regulations or orders
thereunder.

Exemptions

SEC. 13. (a) The Provisions of sections 6 (except section
6(d) in the case of paragraph (1) of this subsection) and 7
shall not apply with respect to—
    (1) any employee employed in a bona fide executive,
administrative or professional capacity (including any employee employed in the capacity of academic administrative
personnel or teacher in elementary or secondary schools),
or in the capacity of outside salesman (as such terms are
defined and delimited from time to time by regulations
of the Secretary, subject to the provisions of the Administrative Procedure Act, except that an employee of a retail
or service establishment shall not be excluded from the
definition of employee employed in a bona fide executive
or administrative capacity because of the number of hours
in his workweek which he devotes to activities not directly
or closely related to the performance of executive or administrative activities, if less than 40 per centum of his hours

worked in the workweek are devoted to such activities); or

(2) any employee employed by any retail or service establishment (except an establishment or employee engaged in laundering, cleaning, or repairing clothing or fabrics or an establishment engaged in the operation of a hospital, institution, or school described in section 3(s)(5)), if more than 50 per centum of such establishment's annual dollar volume of sales of goods or services is made within the State in which the establishment is located, and such establishment is not in an enterprise described in section 3(s). A "retail or service establishment" shall mean an establishment 75 per centum of whose annual dollar volume of sales of goods or services (or of both) is not for resale and is recognized as retail sales in the particular industry; or

(3) any employee employed by an establishment which is an amusement or recreational establishment, organized camp, or religious or non-profit educational conference center, if (A) it does not operate for more than seven months in any calendar year, or (B) during the preceding calendar year, its average receipts for any six months of such year were not more than 33 1/3 per centum of its average receipts for the other six months of such year, except that the exemption from sections 6 and 7 provided by this paragraph does not apply with respect to any employee of a private entity engaged in providing services or facilities (other than, in the case of the exemption from section 6, a private entity engaged in providing services and facilities directly related to skiing) in a national park or a national forest, or on land in the national Wildlife Refuge System, under a contract with the Secretary of the Interior or the Secretary of Agriculture; or

(4) any employee employed by an establishment which qualifies as an exempt retail establishment under clause (2) of this subsection and is recognized as a retail establishment in the particular industry notwithstanding that such establishment makes or processes at the retail establishment the goods that it sells: Provided, That more than 85 per centum of such establishment's annual dollar volume of sales of goods so made or processed is made within the State in which the establishment is located; or

(5) any employee employed in the catching, taking, propagating, harvesting, cultivating, or farming of any kind of fish, shellfish, crustacea, sponges, seaweeds, or other aquatic forms of animal and vegetable life, or in the first processing, canning or packing such marine products at sea as an incident to, or in conjunction with, such fishing opera-

tions, including the going to and returning from work and loading and unloading when performed by any such employee; or

(6) any employee employed in agriculture (A) if such employee is employed by an employer who did not, during any calendar quarter during the preceding calendar year, use more than five hundred man-days of agricultural labor, (B) if such employee is the parent, spouse, child, or other member of his employer's immediate family, (C) if such employee (i) is employed as a hand harvest laborer and is paid on a piece rate basis in an operation which has been, and is customarily and generally recognized as having been, paid on a piece rate basis in the region of employment, (ii) commutes daily from his permanent residence to the farm on which he is so employed, and (iii) has been employed in agriculture less than thirteen weeks during the preceding calendar year, (D) if such employee (other than an employee described in clause (C) of this subsection) (i) is sixteen years of age or under and is employed as a hand harvest laborer, is paid on a piece rate basis in an operation which has been, and is customarily and generally recognized as having been, paid on a piece rate basis in the region of employment, (ii) is employed on the same farm as his parent or person standing in the place of his parent, and (iii) is paid at the same piece rate as employees over age sixteen are paid on the same farm, or (E) if such employee is principally engaged in the range production of livestock; or

(7) any employee to the extent that such employee is exempted by regulations, order, or certificate of the Secretary issued under section 14; or

(8) Any employee employed in connection with the publication of any weekly, semi-weekly, or daily newspaper with a circulation of less than four thousand the major part of which circulation is within the county where published or counties contiguous thereto; or

(9) * * * (Repealed)

[Note: Section 13(a)(9) (relating to motion picture theater employees) was repealed by section 23 of the Fair Labor Standards Amendments of 1974. The 1974 amendments created an exemption for such employees from the overtime provisions only in section 13(b)(27).]

(10) any switchboard operator employed by an independently owned public telephone company which has not more than seven hundred and fifty stations; or

(11) * * * (Repealed)

[Note: Section 13(a)(11) (relating to telegraph agency employees) was repealed by section 10 of the Fair Labor Standards Amendments of 1974. The 1974 amendments created an exemption from the overtime provisions only in section 13(b)(23), which was repealed effective May 1, 1976.]

(12) any employee employed as a seaman on a vessel other than an American vessel; or

(13) * * * (Repealed)

[Note: Section 13(a)(13) (relating to small logging crews) was repealed by section 23 of the Fair Labor Standards Amendments of 1974. The 1974 amendments created an exemption for such employees from the overtime provisions only in section 13(b)(28).]

(14) * * * (Repealed)

[Note: Section 13(a)(14) (relating to employees employed in growing and harvesting of shade grown tobacco) was repealed by section 9 of the Fair Labor Standards Amendments of 1974. The 1974 amendments created an exemption for certain tobacco producing employees from the overtime provisions only in section 13(b)(22). The section 13(b)(22) exemption was repealed, effective January 1, 1978, by section 5 of the Fair Labor Standards Amendments of 1977.]

(15) any employee on a casual basis in domestic service employment to provide babysitting services or any employee employed in domestic service employment to provide companionship services for individuals who (because of age or infirmity) are unable to care for themselves (as such terms are defined and delimited by regulations of the Secretary).

(g) The exemption from section 6 provided by paragraphs (2) and (6) of subsection (a) of this section shall not apply with respect to any employee employed by an establishment (1) which controls, is controlled by, or is under common control with, another establishment the activities of which are not related for a common business purpose to, but materially support the activities of the establishment employing such employee; and (2) whose annual gross volume of sales made or business done, when combined with the annual gross volume of sales made or business done by each establishment which controls, is controlled by, or is under common control with, the establishment employing such employee, exceeds $10,000,000 (exclusive of excise taxes at the retail level which are separately stated), except that the exemption from section 6 provided by paragraph (2) of subsection (a) of this section shall apply with respect to any establishment described in this subsection which has an annual dollar volume of sales which would permit it to qualify for the exemption provided in paragraph (2) of subsection (a) if it were in an enterprise described in section 3(s).

Prohibited Acts

SEC. 15. (a) After the expiration of one hundred and twenty days from the date of enactment of this Act, it shall be unlawful for any person—

(1) to transport, offer for transportation, ship, deliver, or sell in commerce, or to ship, deliver, or sell with knowledge that shipment or delivery or sale thereof in commerce is intended, any goods in the production of which any employee was employed in violation of section 6 or section 7, or in violation of any regulation or order of the Secretary of Labor issued under section 14; except that no provision of this Act shall impose any liability upon any common carrier for the transportation in commerce in the regular course of its business of any goods not produced by such common carrier, and no provision of this Act shall excuse any common carrier from its obligation to accept any goods for transportation; and except that any such transportation, offer, shipment, delivery, or sale of such goods by a purchaser who acquired them in good faith in reliance on written assurance from the producer that the goods were produced in compliance with the requirements of the Act, and who acquired such goods for value without notice of any such violation, shall not be deemed unlawful;

(2) to violate any of the provisions of section 6 or section 7, or any of the provisions of any regulation or order of the Secretary issued under section 14;

(3) to discharge or in any other manner discriminate against any employee because such employee has filed any complaint or instituted or caused to be instituted any proceeding under or related to this Act, or has testified or is about to testify in any such proceeding, or has served or is about to serve on an industry committee;

(4) to violate any of the provisions of section 12;

(5) to violate any of the provisions of section 11(c) or any regulation or order made or continued in effect under the provisions of section 11(d), or to make any statement, report, or record filed or kept pursuant to the provisions of such section or of any regulation or order thereunder, knowing such statement, report, or record to be false in a material respect.

(b) For the purpose of subsection (a)(1) proof that any employee was employed in any place of employment where goods shipped or sold in commerce were produced, within ninety days prior to the removal of the goods from such place of employment, shall be prima facie evidence that such employee was engaged in the production of such goods.

Penalties

SEC. 16. (a) Any person who willfully violates any of the provisions of section 15 shall upon conviction thereof be subject to a fine of not more than $10,000, or to imprisonment for not more than six months, or both. No person shall be imprisoned under this subsection except for an offense committed after the conviction of such person for a prior offense under this subsection.

(b) Any employer who violates the provisions of section 6 or section 7 of this Act shall be liable to the employee or employees affected in the amount of their unpaid minimum wages, or their unpaid overtime compensation, as the case may be, and in an additional equal amount as liquidated damages. Any employer who violates the provisions of section 15(a)(3) of this Act shall be liable for such legal or equitable relief as may be appropriate to effectuate the purposes of section 15(a)(3), including without limitation employment, reinstatement, promotion, and the payment of wages lost and an additional equal amount as liquidated damages. An action to recover the liability prescribed in either of the preceding sentences may be maintained against any employer (including a public agency) in any Federal or State court of competent jurisdiction by any one or more employees for and in behalf of himself or themselves and other employees similarly situated. No employee shall be a party plaintiff to any such action unless he gives his consent in writing to become such a party and such consent is filed in the court in which such action is brought. The court in such action shall, in addition to any judgment awarded to the plaintiff or plaintiffs, allow a reasonable attorney's fee to be paid by the defendant, and costs of the action. The right provided by this subsection to bring an action by or on behalf of any employee, and the right of any employee to become a party plaintiff to any such action, shall terminate upon the filing of a complaint by the Secretary of Labor in an action under section 17 in which (1) restraint is sought of any further delay in the payment of unpaid minimum wages, or the amount of unpaid overtime compensation as the case may be, owing to such employee under section 6 or section 7 of this Act by an employer liable therefore under the provisions of this subsection or (2) legal or equitable relief is sought as a result of alleged violations of section 15(a)(3).

(c) The Secretary is authorized to supervise the payment of the unpaid minimum wages or the unpaid overtime compensation owing to any employee or employees under section 6 or 7 of this Act, and the agreement of any employee to accept such payment shall upon payment in full constitute a waiver by such employee of any right he may have under subsection (b) of this section to such unpaid minimum wages or unpaid overtime compensation and an additional equal amount as liquidated damages. The Secretary may bring an action in any court of competent jurisdiction to recover the amount of the unpaid minimum wages or overtime compensation and an equal amount as liquidated damages. The right provided by subsection (b) to bring an action by or on behalf of any employee to recover the liability specified in the first sentence of such subsection and of any employee to become a party plaintiff to any such action shall terminate upon the filing of a complaint by the Secretary in an action under this subsection in which a recovery is sought of unpaid minimum wages or unpaid overtime compensation under sections 6 and 7 or liquidated or other damages provided by this subsection owing to such employee by an employer liable under the provisions of subsection (b), unless such action is dismissed without prejudice on motion of the Secretary. Any sums thus recovered by the Secretary on behalf of an employee pursuant to this subsection shall be held in a special deposit account and shall be paid, on order of the Secretary, directly to the employee or employees affected. Any such sums not paid to an employee because of inability to do so within a period of three years shall be covered into the Treasury of the United States as miscellaneous receipts. In determining when an action is commenced by the Secretary under this subsection for the purposes of the statutes of limitations provided in section 6(a) of the Portal-to-Portal Act of 1947, it shall be considered to be commenced in the case of any individual claimant on the date when the complaint is filed if he is specifically named as a party plaintiff in the complaint, or if his name did not so appear, on the subsequent date on which his name is added as a party plaintiff in such action.

(d) In any action or proceeding commenced prior to, on, or after the date of enactment of this subsection, no employer shall be subject to any liability or punishment under this Act or the Portal-to-Portal Act of 1947 or on account of his failure to comply with any provision or provisions of such Acts (1) with respect to work heretofore or hereafter performed in a workplace to which the exemption in section 13(f) is applicable, (2) with respect to work performed in Guam, the Canal Zone or Wake Island before the effective date of this amendment of subsection (d), or (3) with respect to work performed in a possession named in section 6(a)(3) at any time prior to the establishment by the Secretary, as provided therein, of a minimum wage rate applicable to such work.

Injunction Proceedings

SEC. 17. The district courts, together with the United States District Court for the District of the Canal Zone, the District Court of the Virgin Islands, and the District Court of Guam shall have jurisdiction, for cause shown, to restrain violations of section 15, including in the case of violations of section 15(a)(2) the restraint of any withholding of payment of minimum wages or overtime compensation found by the court to be due to employees under this Act (except sums which employees are barred from recovering, at the time of the commencement of the action to restrain the violations, by virtue of the provisions of section 6 of the Portal-to-Portal Act of 1947).

Relation to Other Laws

SEC. 18. (a) No provision of this Act or of any order thereunder shall excuse noncompliance with any Federal or State law or municipal ordinance establishing a minimum wage higher than the minimum wage established under this Act or a maximum workweek lower than the maximum workweek established under this Act, and no provision of this Act relating to the employment of child labor shall justify noncompliance with any Federal or State law or municipal ordinance establishing a higher standard than the standard established under this Act. No provision of this Act shall justify any employer in reducing a wage paid by him which is in excess of the applicable minimum wage under this Act, or justify any employer in increasing hours of employment maintained by him which are shorter than the maximum hours applicable under this Act.

Separability of Provisions

SEC. 19. If any provision of this Act or the application of such provision to any person or circumstances is held invalid, the remainder of the Act and the application of such provision to other persons or circumstances shall not be affected thereby.

Approved, June 25, 1938.

In the following excerpts from the Portal-to-Portal Act of 1947, the authority given to the Secretary of Labor is exercised by the Equal Employment Opportunity Commission for purposes of enforcing the Equal Pay Act of 1963.

Part IV—Miscellaneous

SEC. 6. STATUTE OF LIMITATIONS.—Any action commenced
on or after the date of the enactment of this Act to enforce
any cause of action for unpaid minimum wages, unpaid overtime compensation, or liquidated damages, under the Fair
Labor Standards Act of 1938, as amended, the Walsh-Healey
Act, or the Bacon-Davis Act—
(a) if the cause of action accrues on or after the date of
the enactment of this Act—may be commenced within two
years after the cause of action accrued, and every such
action shall be forever barred unless commenced within
two years after the cause of action accrued, except that
a cause of action arising out of a willful violation may be
commenced within three years after the cause of action
accrued;

SEC. 7. DETERMINATION OF COMMENCEMENT OF FUTURE
ACTIONS.—In determining when an action is commenced
for the purposes of section 6, an action commenced on or
after the date of the enactment of this Act under the Fair
Labor Standards Act of 1938, as amended, the Walsh-Healey
Act, or the Bacon-Davis Act, shall be considered to be commenced on the date when the complaint is filed; except
that in the case of a collective or class action instituted
under the Fair Labor Standards Act of 1938, as amended,
or the Bacon-Davis Act, it shall be considered to be commenced in the case of any individual claimant—
(a) on the date when the complaint is filed, if he is specifically
named as a party plaintiff in the complaint and his written
consent to become a party plaintiff is filed on such date
in the court in which the action is brought; or
(b) if such written consent was not so filed or if his name
did not so appear—on the subsequent date on which such
written consent is filed in the court in which the action
was commenced.

SEC. 10. RELIANCE IN FUTURE ON ADMINISTRATIVE
RULINGS, ETC.—
(a) In any action or proceeding based on any act or omission
on or after the date of the enactment of this Act, no employer
shall be subject to any liability or punishment for or on account of the failure of the employer to pay minimum wages
or overtime compensation under the Fair Labor Standards
Act of 1938, as amended, the Walsh-Healey Act, or the
Bacon-Davis Act, if he pleads and proves that the act of
omission complained of was in good faith in conformity

with and reliance on any written administrative regulation, order, ruling, approval, or interpretation, of the agency of the United States specified in subsection (b) of this section, or any administrative practice or enforcement policy of such agency with respect to the class of employers to which he belonged. Such a defense, if established, shall be a bar to the action or proceeding, notwithstanding that after such act or omission, such administrative regulation, order, ruling, approval, interpretation, practice, or enforcement policy is modified or rescinded or is determined by judicial authority to be invalid or of no legal effect.

(b) The agency referred to in subsection (a) shall be—

(1) in the case of the Fair Labor Standards Act of 1938, as amended—the Secretary of Labor;

SEC. 11. LIQUIDATED DAMAGES.—In any action commenced prior to or on or after the date of the enactment of this Act to recover unpaid minimum wages, unpaid overtime compensation, or liquidated damages, under the Fair Labor Standards Act of 1938, as amended, if the employer shows to the satisfaction of the court that the act or omission giving rise to such action was in good faith and that he had reasonable grounds for believing that his act or omission was not a violation of the Fair Labor Standards Act of 1938, as amended, the court may, in its sound discretion, award no liquidated damages or award any amount thereof not to exceed the amount specified in section 16 of such Act.

SEC. 13. DEFINITIONS.—

(a) When the terms "employer", "employee", and "wage" are used in this Act in relation to the Fair Labor Standards Act of 1938, as amended, they shall have the same meaning as when used in such Act of 1938.

SEC. 14. SEPARABILITY.—If any provision of this Act or the application of such provision to any person or circumstance is held invalid, the remainder of this Act and the application of such provision to other persons or circumstances shall not be affected thereby.

SEC. 15. SHORT TITLE.—This Act may be cited as the "Portal-to-Portal Act of 1947".

Approved May 14, 1947.

Appendix D

Comparison Between Title VII, Equal Pay Act and Age Discrimination in Employment Act

Issue	Title VII	EPA	ADEA
1. Number of employees required for jurisdiction	15	2, but male and female employees need not be employed simultaneously	20, except no number required where public employer
2. Charge	required	none required	not required, except for individual action
3. Notice to employer of charge or complaint	required	none required	not required for Commission action; required for protection of individual rights
4. Anonymity of charging or complaining party	impossible since copy of charge must be served; can be achieved by using commission charge	required unless employee waives	required where complaint only — name given where charge filed
5. Deferral to state agency	required	not required	not required
6. Finding of reasonable cause	required before EEOC can sue	not required	not required
7. Conciliation	effort required only for Commission suit	not required	effort required only for Commission suit

Issue	Title VII	EPA	ADEA
8. Statute of limitations	180 or 300 days for filing of charge, which then tolls statute, back pay may be received for 2 years prior to charge	3 years if willful; 2 years if not willful; statute not tolled until suit filed	Commission suit: 2 years, 3 if willful; tolled for up to 1 year for conciliation after notice. Private suit: 2 years, 3 if willful, but charge must be filed within 180 or 300 days
9. Jury trial	never possible	if filed under Section 16 (c) either Commission or employer is entitled to jury; jury possible in all private actions	same as EPA
10. Cutting off private rights by filing of suit by Commission	does not occur	all employees, whether specifically named or otherwise embraced within the group on behalf of whom Commission sues, lose all private rights as soon as the Commission files suit, unless they have previously instituted action	same as EPA
11. Right of charging or complaining party to intervene in suit filed by Commission	court has discretion to permit	never possible	same as EPA

Issue	Title VII	EPA	ADEA
12. Who can be sued as an employer	"any agent" of a covered employer	"any person acting directly or indirectly in the interest of any employer in relation to an employee"	any covered employer
13. Union as defendant	named as defendant wherever charged and reasonable cause found; otherwise named as Fed. R.Civ.P. 19 defendant	named only as Fed.R.Civ.P. 19 defendant	named as defendant whenever union violates prohibitions of 29 U.S.C. 623(c); otherwise named as Fed.R.Civ.P. 19 defendant
14. Same establishment	may be based on a comparison of wages of males with females who do not work in the same establishment	male and female must work in the same establishment in order to establish a violation	not applicable
15. Liquidated damages	never possible	amount equal to damages may be assessed, if action brought under 16(b) or 16(c), in the discretion of the court	amount equal to damages may be assessed if action brought under 16(b) or 16(c) and a willful violation is alleged and proved
16. Mandatory compensatory damages	all monetary relief is subject to discretion of court although back pay should usually be awarded where discrimination causes loss	court has no discretion to fail to award difference in pay between male and female	same as Title VII
17. Monetary award for employees who are deceased or cannot be found	never available unless estate of employee available to receive money	cannot be returned to employer but must be paid into United States Treasury of clerk of court	same as EPA

Issue	Title VII	EPA	ADEA
18. Public employers other than the United States	Commission cannot sue but must refer to Department of Justice which is empowered to bring suit	Commission can sue	Commission can sue
19. Directed Investigation (right to investigate where no charge)	Only on Commission charge	any time	any time

Appendix E
Charge Forms

CHARGE OF DISCRIMINATION	ENTER CHARGE NUMBER
This form is affected by the Privacy Act of 1974; see Privacy Act Statement on reverse before completing this form.	☐ FEPA ☒ EEOC

(Sample)

_____ and EEOC
(State or local Agency, if any)

NAME *(Indicate Mr., Ms., or Mrs.)* Ms. Sheilah James	HOME TELEPHONE NO. *(Include Area Code)* (215) 666-1212

STREET ADDRESS 165 Hamford Circle	CITY, STATE AND ZIP CODE Aspen, Colorado 80389	COUNTY Arapahoe

NAMED IS THE EMPLOYER, LABOR ORGANIZATION, EMPLOYMENT AGENCY, APPRENTICESHIP COMMITTEE, STATE OR LOCAL GOVERNMENT AGENCY WHO DISCRIMINATED AGAINST ME *(If more than one list below.)*

NAME Buffalo Works, Inc.	NO. OF EMPLOYEES/MEMBERS 100	TELEPHONE NUMBER *(Include Area Code)* (215) 655-0900

STREET ADDRESS 247 River Road	CITY, STATE AND ZIP CODE Glenwood, Colorado 80167

NAME	TELEPHONE NUMBER *(Include Area Code)*

STREET ADDRESS	CITY, STATE AND ZIP CODE

CAUSE OF DISCRIMINATION BASED ON *(Check appropriate box(es))* ☒ RACE ☐ COLOR ☒ SEX ☐ RELIGION ☐ NATIONAL ORIGIN ☐ AGE ☐ RETALIATION ☐ OTHER*(Specify)*	DATE MOST RECENT OR CONTINUING DISCRIMINATION TOOK PLACE *(Month, day, year)* 9/29/88

THE PARTICULARS ARE *(If additional space is needed, attached extra sheet(s)):*

1. I was hired as a laborer on May 18, 1984.

2. In July 1988, I was told that there would be a reduction in staffing and my job would be eliminated.

3. On July 29, I learned that Skip Bell and Jeff Orr, both white males, would be retained.

4. On September 29, I was terminated. I had more experience than Bell or Orr who remained on the job. I believe I was discriminated against because of my race, Black, and sex, Female.

☐ I also want this charge filed with the EEOC. I will advise the agencies if I change my address or telephone number and I will cooperate fully with them in the processing of my charge in accordance with their procedures.	NOTARY - (When necessary to meet State and Local Requirements) I swear or affirm that I have read the above charge and that it is true to the best of my knowledge, information and belief.
I declare under penalty of perjury that the foregoing is true and correct.	SIGNATURE OF COMPLAINANT
10/1/88 Date *Sheilah James* Charging Party *(Signature)*	SUBSCRIBED AND SWORN TO BEFORE ME THIS DATE (Day, month, and year)

EEOC FORM 5 MAR 84   PREVIOUS EDITIONS OF THIS FORM ARE OBSOLETE AND MUST NOT BE USED

FILE COPY

US EQUAL EMPLOYMENT OPPORTUNITY COMMISSION

INFORMATION SHEET FOR CHARGING PARTIES AND COMPLAINANTS

EEOC PROCEDURES:

The Equal Employment Opportunity Commission (EEOC) will investigate the allegations you have made. The EEOC investigator will ask you questions, will ask the respondent questions, may ask witnesses questions, and may review records. Based on the evidence gathered, the investigator will prepare a recommended determination for the Office Director on whether discrimination has occurred. You will be given a Letter of Determination which will state whether there is reason or not to believe that discrimination has occurred. If you have filed a complaint, rather than a charge, or if you have had a charge filed on your behalf, your identity as a complainant will be kept in confidence throughout EEOC's handling of your case.

° If the Director believes that the allegations you have made are supported by the evidence, the Letter of Determination will say this and will ask the respondent to meet with EEOC and work out an agreement which will provide relief for the harm caused by the discrimination. If an agreement cannot be worked out, the investigation file will be reviewed in EEOC Headquarters and EEOC (or the Department of Justice in some cases) will either sue on your behalf or notify you of your right to sue (see information below about Your Private Suit Rights).

° If the Director believes that some or all of the allegations in your charge are not supported by the evidence, the Letter of Determination will say this and will notify you of your right to request EEOC Headquarters review of the Determination and of the date that the Determination will become final if you do not request review. A Request for Review Form will be sent to you with the Letter of Determination.

If you do not request review within 14 days of the Determination, it will become EEOC's final determination on the 15th day and the investigation will be ended. You can then decide if you want to file a private lawsuit to enforce your rights in court (see the information below about Your Private Suit Rights).

If you request EEOC Headquarters review of the Determination within 14 days, and your request is accepted, a final EEOC Determination will be sent to you after the review is complete. This Determination will notify you if EEOC will take any further action and the effect on your private suit rights.

YOUR RESPONSIBILITIES:

Please inform EEOC of any prolonged absence from home or change of your address. Please claim any certified mail which EEOC may send you. If EEOC cannot locate you or if EEOC asks you to do something necessary to its investigation, and you decline to do so, EEOC may notify you that the investigation will be discontinued and notify you of your right to sue (see the information below about Your Private Suit Rights). You may retain a lawyer while your case is investigated, but you are not required to do so.

YOUR PRIVATE SUIT RIGHTS UNDER TITLE VII:

If you filed a charge with EEOC under Title VII of the Civil Rights Act, you have preserved your right to sue the respondent named in your charge. If we cannot resolve your charge, we will notify you of your right to sue. You may then file a lawsuit in U.S. District Court within 90 days from receipt of our Notice in order to enforce your rights in court. Once this 90 day period is over, your right to sue is lost. EEOC may give you notice of your right to sue in the following circumstances:

° If You Ask for a Notice of Right to Sue. You may not wish to wait for EEOC to complete its investigation or your attorney may recommend that you file your own lawsuit. You can obtain a Notice of Right to Sue in such cases by asking the Office where you filed your charge to issue a Notice to you, even though our investigation is not finished. If you ask, EEOC will issue a Notice to you after 180 days have passed from the date you filed your charge. In some cases, if you ask, we will issue the Notice to you at an earlier time, if it is known that the investigation will take a long time to complete. You will have 90 days to file suit from the day you receive the Notice of Right to Sue.

° If EEOC Finds No Violation with Respect to All the Allegations in Your Charge. Before this happens, you will be interviewed by EEOC and given an opportunity to provide additional evidence. If, at the end of investigation, you are given a

Letter of Determination stating that there are no violations, you will be told that you may, within 14 days, ask EEOC Headquarters to review the Determination. You will have 90 days to file suit from the day a determination in your case becomes final -- either after the 14 day period is over if you do not ask for a review or after final EEOC action at a later date if you do ask for a review.

* **If EEOC Finds a Violation, Fails to Obtain Relief, and Decides Not to Sue on Your Behalf.** If EEOC finds a violation but does not succeed in obtaining relief under the law, the investigation is reviewed by EEOC's Commissioners to decide if a lawsuit will be filed. Sometimes the Commissioners decide that a lawsuit will not be filed. If this happens, you will be notified and receive a Notice of Right to Sue. You will have 90 days to file suit from the day you receive the Notice.

* **If Your Charge is Dismissed.** EEOC Regulations require a charge to be dismissed when (1) an investigation shows that the law does not apply to your case, (2) when it is not possible to continue the investigation due to an inability to locate you, (3) because you did not cooperate in some way necessary to the investigation, or (4) you did not accept a settlement offer which afforded you full relief for the harm which you alleged. EEOC may discontinue its investigation by notifying you that it has dismissed your charge. You will have 90 days to file suit from the day you receive the Notice of Right to Sue.

YOUR PRIVATE SUIT RIGHTS UNDER THE AGE DISCRIMINATION IN EMPLOYMENT ACT (ADEA) OR EQUAL PAY ACT (EPA):

If you filed a charge or complaint under the ADEA or EPA, the above rules on your private suit rights do not apply. However, as stated on the reverse side under "EEOC Procedures", you may request an EEOC Headquarters review of a no violation finding under these laws. Please note that such a request for review will not extend the time you have for filing a lawsuit. You must file suit within two years of the alleged discrimination (three years in cases of willful violations). You must wait 60 days from the day you filed an ADEA charge before you can sue under that law.

If you have any questions, please call the EEOC office which last handled your case.

Appendix F
EEOC Field Offices

Albuquerque Area Office
505 Marquette, N.W., Suite 1105
Albuquerque, New Mexico 87102-2189
(Hours - 7:30 a.m. - 4:30 p.m. MST)

(Phoenix District)

505-766-2061

Atlanta District Office
75 Piedmont Avenue, N.E., Suite 1100
Atlanta, Georgia 30335
(Hours - 8:30 a.m. - 5:00 p.m. EST)

404-331-6093

Baltimore District Office
109 Market Place, Suite 4000
Baltimore, Maryland 21202
(Hours - 9:00 a.m. - 5:30 p.m. EST)

301-962-3932

Birmingham District Office
2121 Eighth Avenue, North, Suite 824
Birmingham, Alabama 35203
(Hours - 8:00 a.m. - 4:30 p.m. CST)

205-731-0082

Boston Area Office
JFK Federal Building, Room 409-B
Boston, Massachusetts 02203
(Hours - 8:30 a.m. - 5:00 p.m. EST)

(New York District)

617-565-3200

Buffalo Local Office
28 Church Street, Room 301
Buffalo, New York 14202
(Hours - 8:45 a.m. - 5:15 p.m. EST)

(New York District)

716-846-4441

Charlotte District Office
5500 Central Avenue
Charlotte, North Carolina 28212   704-567-7100
   (Hours - 8:30 a.m. - 5:00 p.m. EST)

Chicago District Office
536 South Clark Street, Room 930-A
Chicago, Illinois 60605   312-353-2713
   (Hours - 8:30 a.m. - 5:00 p.m. CST)

Cincinnati Area Office   (Cleveland District)
550 Main Street, Room 7015
Cincinnati, Ohio 45202   513-684-2851
   (Hours - 8:15 a.m. - 5:00 p.m. EST)

Cleveland District Office
1375 Euclid Avenue, Room 600
Cleveland, Ohio 44115   216-522-2001
   (Hours 8:15 a.m. - 5:00 p.m. EST)

Dallas District Office
8303 Elmbrook Drive
Dallas, Texas 75247   214-767-7015
   (Hours - 8:30 a.m. - 5:00 p.m. CST)

Denver District Office
1845 Sherman Street, 2nd Floor
Denver, Colorado 80203   303-866-1300
   (Hours - 8:00 a.m. - 5:00 p.m. MST)

Detroit District Office
477 Michigan Avenue, Room 1540
Detroit, Michigan 48226   313-226-7636
   (Hours - 8:30 a.m. - 5:00 p.m. EST)

El Paso Area Office   (San Antonio District)
700 East San Antonio Street, Room B-406
El Paso, Texas 79901   915-534-6550
   (Hours - 8:30 a.m. - 5:00 p.m. CST)

Fresno Local Office   (San Francisco District)
1313 P Street, Suite 103
Fresno, California 93721   209-487-5793
   (Hours - 8:00 a.m. - 5:00 p.m. PST)

Greensboro Local Office   (Charlotte District)
324 West Market Street, Room B-27
P.O. Box 3363
Greensboro, North Carolina 27401   919-333-5174
   (Hours - 8:30 a.m. - 5:00 p.m. EST)

Greenville Local Office   (Charlotte District)
211 Century Drive, Suite 109-B
Greenville, South Carolina 29607   803-233-1791
   (Hours - 8:30 a.m. - 5:00 p.m. EST)

Honolulu Local Office   (San Francisco District)
300 Ala Moana Blvd., Room 3316-A
P.O. Box 50082
Honolulu, Hawaii 96850   808-541-3120
   (Hours - 8:00 a.m. - 5:00 p.m. HAT*)
*Time is Hawaiian Aleutian Time and is 6 hours behind EST

Houston District Office
405 Main Street, 6th Floor
Houston, Texas 77002   713-226-2601
   (Hours - 8:00 a.m. - 5:00 p.m. CST)

Indianapolis District Office
46 East Ohio Street, Room 456
Indianapolis, Indiana 46204   317-269-7212
   (Hours - 8:00 a.m. - 4:30 p.m. EST)

Jackson Area Office   (Birmingham District)
100 West Capitol Street, Suite 721
Jackson, Mississippi 39269   601-965-4537
   (Hours - 8:00 a.m. - 4:30 p.m. CST)

Kansas City Area Office   (St. Louis District)
911 Walnut, 10th Floor
Kansas City, Missouri 64106   816-426-5773
   (Hours - 8:00 a.m. - 4:30 p.m. CST)

Little Rock Area Office   (Memphis District)
320 West Capitol Avenue, Suite 621
Little Rock, Arkansas 72201   501-378-5060
   (Hours - 8:00 a.m. - 4:30 p.m. CST)

Los Angeles District Office
3660 Wilshire Blvd., 5th Floor
Los Angeles, California 90010   213-251-7278
   (Hours - 8:30 a.m. - 5:00 p.m. PST)

Louisville Area Office   (Indianapolis District)
601 West Broadway, Room 613
Louisville, Kentucky 40202   502-582-6082
    (Hours - 8:00 a.m. - 4:30 p.m. EST)

Newark Area Office   (Philadelphia District)
60 Park Place, Room 301
Newark, New Jersey 07102   201-645-6383
    (Hours - 8:00 a.m. - 4:30 p.m. EST)

New Orleans District Office
701 Loyola Avenue, Suite 600
New Orleans, Louisiana 70113   504-589-2329
    (Hours - 8:00 a.m. - 4:30 p.m. CST)

New York District Office
90 Church Street, Room 1501
New York, New York 10007   212-264-7161
    (Hours - 8:45 a.m. - 5:15 p.m. EST)

Norfolk Area Office   (Baltimore District)
200 Granby Mall, Room 412
Norfolk, Virginia 23510   804-441-3470
    (Hours - 8:30 a.m. - 5:00 p.m. EST)

Oakland Local Office   (San Francisco District)
1333 Broadway, Room 430
Oakland, California 94612   415-273-7588
    (Hours - 8:00 a.m. - 4:30 p.m. PST)

Oklahoma Area Office   (Dallas District)
200 N.W. 5th Street, Room 703
Oklahoma City, Oklahoma 73102   405-231-4911
    (Hours - 8:00 a.m. - 5:00 p.m. CST)

Philadelphia District Office
1421 Cherry Street, 10th Floor
Philadelphia, Pennsylvania 19102   215-597-7784
    (Hours - 8:00 a.m. - 4:30 p.m. EST)

Phoenix District Office
4520 N. Central Avenue, Suite 300
Phoenix, Arizona 85012-1848   602-261-3882
    (Hours - 8:00 a.m. - 5:00 p.m. MST)

Pittsburgh Area Office	(Philadelphia District)
1000 Liberty Avenue, Room 2038-A	
Pittsburgh, Pennsylvania 15222	412-644-3444
(Hours - 8:00 a.m. - 4:30 p.m. EST)	

Raleigh Area Office   (Charlotte District)
127 West Hargett Street, Suite 500
Raleigh, North Carolina 27601   919-856-4064
(Hours - 8:30 a.m. - 5:00 p.m. EST)

Richmond Area Office   (Baltimore District)
400 North 8th Street, Room 7026
Richmond, Virginia 23240   804-771-2692
(Hours - 8:30 a.m. - 5:00 p.m. EST)

San Antonio District Office
5410 Fredericksburg Road, Suite 200
San Antonio, Texas 78229   512-229-4810
(Hours - 8:30 a.m. - 5:00 p.m. CST)

San Diego Local Office   (Los Angeles District)
880 Front Street, Room 4S-21
San Diego, California 92188   619-293-6288
(Hours - 8:30 a.m. - 5:00 p.m. PST)

San Francisco District Office
901 Market Street, Suite 500
San Francisco, California 94103   415-995-5049
(Hours - 8:30 a.m. - 5:00 p.m. PST)

San Jose Local Office   (San Francisco District)
280 South First Street, Room 4150
San Jose, California 95113   408-291-7352
(Hours - 8:30 a.m. - 5:00 p.m. CST)

Savannah Local Office   (Atlanta District)
10 Whitaker Street, Suite B
Savannah, Georgia 31401   912-944-4234
(Hours 8:30 a.m. - 5:00 p.m. EST)

Seattle District Office
1321 Second Avenue, 7th Floor
Seattle, Washington 98101   206-442-0968
(Hours - 8:30 a.m. - 5:00 p.m. PST)

St. Louis District Office
625 N. Euclid Street, 5th Floor
St. Louis, Missouri 63108   314-425-6585
    (Hours - 8:00 a.m. - 4:30 p.m. CST)

Tampa Area Office   (Miami District)
700 Twiggs Street, Room 302
Tampa, Florida 33602   813-228-2310
    (Hours - 8:00 a.m. - 4:30 p.m. EST)

Washington Area Office   (Baltimore District)
1717 H Street, N.W., Suite 400
Washington, D.C. 20006   202-653-6197
    (Hours - 9:00 a.m. - 5:30 p.m. EST)

Case Index

Broderick v. Ruder, 685 F. Supp. 1269 (D.D.C. 1988) 75
Craft v. Metromedia, 575 F. Supp. 868 (W.D. Mo. 1983) 90
Doe v. St. Joseph's Hospital of Fort Wayne, 788 F. 2d 411 (7th Cir. 1986) 12
Dothard v. Rawlinson, 433 U.S. 321 (1977) 23, 86
Espinoza v. Farah Manufacturing Co., Inc., 414 U.S. 86 (1973) 68
Griggs v. Duke Power Co., 401 U.S. 424 (1971) 51, 52, 53, 57, 59
Hazelwood Indep. School Dist. v. United States, 433 U.S. 299 (1977) 55
International Brotherhood of Teamsters v. United States, 431 U.S. 324 (1977) 27
Lemons v. City and County of Denver, 620 F. 2d 228 (10th Cir. 1980) 94
McDonnell Douglas v. Green, 411 U.S. 792 (1973) 34, 35, 36, 41, 66
McLaughlin v. Richland Shoe Co., 108 S. Ct. 1677 (1988) 103
Mares v. Marsh, 777 F. 2d 1066 (5th Cir. 1985) 12
Quijano v. University Federal Credit Union, 617 F. 2d 129 (5th Cir. 1980) 15-16
Trans World Airlines v. Hardison, 432 U.S. 63 (1977) 81
Trans World Airlines v. Thurston, 469 U.S. 111 (1985) 111
United Air Lines v. Evans, 431 U.S. 553 (1977) 105
United States v. Seeger, 380 U.S. 163 (1965) 80
Watson v. Fort Worth Bank and Trust, 108 S. Ct. 2777 (1988) 53, 61, 62
Welsh v. United States, 398 U.S. 333 (1970) 80

Index

abortion 79
advisors 13
affirmative action: elements 84; goals 85; non-minority rights 85-86; past acts 83; reasonable action 84-85; reasonable basis 84; reductions-in-force 86; self analysis 84; seniority systems 28-29
age: employer's knowledge 50; prima facie case 71-72; protected ages 7, 13; reduction-in-force 71-73
Age Discrimination Claims Assistance Act 103-104
Age Discrimination in Employment Act 6-9; BFOQ 24-26; purpose 6-7; seniority systems 29-30
agriculture: EPA 10
applications 11, 124
apprenticeships 20
attorney's fees 36

benefit plans 30-32
Bona Fide Occupational Qualification (BFOQ): ADEA 24-26; color 21; firefighters 25; hospitals 23; national origin 24; nursing homes 23; pilots 26; police officers 25; prisons 23; profanity 22; race 20-21; religion 24; role models 22; school bus drivers 26; sex 21
bumping: ADEA 72-73
business necessity 51-52, 56-58

causation 39, 42
charges: filing 115-116; timeliness-EPA 10; timeliness-Title VII 6
churches see religious institutions
citizenship 67-69
Civil Rights Act of 1866 68
civil service 13
Communist Party 16
comparable worth 94
conciliation 118
continuing violations 105-106
credit unions 15-16

damages: back pay 109-110; EPA 112-113; front pay 109-110; liquidated 111-112; liquidated-ADEA 7-8, 111-112; liquidated-EPA 9-10, 112-113; mitigation 110; pensions 110; reinstatement

110-111; reinstatement offers
110; Section 1981 66; Section
1983 66; severance pay 110;
social security 110; timing 46;
unemployment 110
disparate impact 51-62; ADEA
59-61; alternatives 52, 58-
59; applicants 54; neutral
policy 53
disparate treatment 33-50;
ADEA 41-43; evidence 43-50;
evidentiary burdens 34-40;
intent 33-34; Title VII 33-40
dress codes: business 90-92;
religious reason 82-83
dressing rooms 24

early retirement 127-128 **see
also** reductions-in-force
educational institutions: employer 5
employees: definition 11-13;
minimum number-ADEA 8,
13, 14; minimum number-
EPA 10; minimum number-
Title VII 5, 13
employers 13-14; ADEA 14;
Title VII 13
employer's response: ADEA 41;
good faith 40; nondiscriminatory response 34, 36-38
employment agencies 5-6, 8, 9
Equal Employment Opportunity
Commission: administration
115-118; attorney-of-the-
day 118; authority 5; interpretations 17-18; investigations 6, 9, 117
Equal Pay Act 9; effort 93-94;
establishment 95; merit system 92-93; responsibility 93-
94; seniority 92-93; skill 93-
94
evaluations 40, 43-44, 72, 126-
127

executives: ADEA 18-19
experts 55

federal employees: age 121;
equal pay 121; filing complaints 119-120; filing lawsuits 121-122; hearings 120-
121; procedures 119-122
firefighters 25
fishing: EPA 10

grooming 88-92

hair: facial 89-90; head 88-89;
religious reason 83
height 86-88; minimums 86, 87
high school diploma 51, 52, 53,
57
hospitals 23
hostile environment 63-65, 75-
76

Immigration Reform and Control
Act 68-69
independent contractors 11
Indian reservations 16-17
intelligence tests 51, 53
interviews 124-125
involuntary retirement 32;
seniority systems 29

jury trials: ADEA 7-8; EPA
10; Section 1981 66; Sec-
tion 1983 66
juvenile rehabilitation: BFOQ
22

labor organizations 5, 8-9
lawsuits: timeliness **see**
statute of limitations
life insurance 31
liquidated damages **see** damages

local governments: employer 5
long-term disability 31-32

maternity leave 78
medical insurance 31, 77
mergers: seniority systems 29
ministers 15

national origin 67-71; BFOQ 24
national security 17
newspapers: EPA 10
nursing homes 23

objective criteria 37, 38

pattern and practice 61-62
performance 35
pilots 26
police officers 25
policymakers 13, 19
posters 106-107
pregnancy 77-79; fetal pro-
    tection 79; maternity
    leave 78; medical insur-
    ance 77; sick leave 77-78;
    single mothers 79
Pregnancy Discrimination Act
    77-79
pretext: ADEA 41; Title VII 34,
    38-40
prevention 123-131; applica-
    tions 124; early retirement
    plans 127-128; evaluations
    126; interviews 124; paper-
    work 123-124; sexual harass-
    ment 128-131; waivers/re-
    leases 127-128
prima facie case: ADEA 41;
    reduction-in-force 71-72;

Title VII 34, 35-36
prior acts 45
prisons 23
privacy: BFOQ 23-24
private membership organiza-
    tions 15-16
profanity: BFOQ 22
protected groups: sexual harass-
    ment 74-75; Title VII 5, 35
pseudo-folliculitis barbae 89-90

qualifications 35-36, 39

race 63-67
racial harassment 63-65; Sec-
    tion 1981 67
racial slurs 63-65
reduction-in-force: affirmative
    action 86; prima facie case
    71-72
releases see waivers/releases
religious accommodation 79-83;
    flexible scheduling 81; over-
    time 81; seniority systems 81;
    substitutions 80-81
religious beliefs 79-80
religious institutions 14-15;
    BFOQ 24; education 14-15;
    non-profit activity 14; reli-
    gious activity 14
retail sales: EPA 10
retaliation 95-98; employer
    knowledge 96-97; executives
    97; prima facie 96
right-to-sue letters 6, 101-102

Sabbaths 80
salaries 73-74
school bus drivers 26
Section 1981 65-67
Section 1983 65-67

seniority systems 26-30; ADEA
   29-30; affirmative action 28-
   29; involuntary retirement
   29; mergers 29; Title VII 26-
   29
sexual harassment 74-76, 128-
   131; dress codes 91; employer
   knowledge 75; sexual advances 76; state court actions 76
similarly situated 36
speak-English-only rules 69-
   71
state governments: employer
   5
state laws: supremacy clause
   22
statements: offensive 48-50
statistics 54-55, 58-59
statute of limitations 99-107;
   ADEA 102-104; continuing
   violations 105-106; employee
   knowledge 99-100; EPA 10,
   104; federal employees 119-
   122; misrepresentations 100;
   Section 1981 66-67; Section 1983 66-67; Title VII
   6, 101-103
stereotypes: sex 21-22

subjective criteria 37, 38, 53-
   54, 126-127

teaching faculty 20
Title VII of Civil Rights Act of
   1964 5-6; charge 6
titles (position) 47

unions see labor organizations
United States: employer 5

validity studies 56-58, 59
veterans 17

wages: sex-based 92
waivers/releases 127-128
warnings 47-48
weight 86-88; maximums 88;
   minimums 87-88
willful violations: ADEA 103,
   111-112; EPA 112-113